Meet and Write

book two

Monique Pirie

Lost on May 1st and
found on May 2nd !
Where was it ???!

Meet and Write

A teaching anthology of contemporary poetry
in three books

book one
book two
book three

Meet and Write

A teaching anthology of contemporary poetry

book two

Edited by Sandy and Alan Brownjohn

HODDER AND STOUGHTON

LONDON SYDNEY AUCKLAND TORONTO

British Library Cataloguing in Publication Data
  Meet and write: a teaching anthology of contemporary poetry.
  Bk. 2.
  1. English poetry——20th century
  I. Brownjohn, Sandy   II. Brownjohn, Alan
  821'.914'08   PR1174

  ISBN 0 340 37150 1

First published 1987

Printed and bound in Great Britain for
Hodder and Stoughton Educational,
a division of Hodder and Stoughton Ltd,
Mill Road, Dunton Green, Sevenoaks, Kent,
by Page Bros (Norwich) Ltd.

Contents

How to Get the Most Out of This Book

Meet and Write is intended to introduce you to the work of modern poets, and at the same time to encourage you to explore the techniques and the crafts of poetry by writing yourself.

There are twelve poets represented in Book Two and each poet has written a personal introduction to the section containing his/her work. At the end of each section there is a brief discussion of the poems, and explanations of the techniques used. There are plenty of suggestions to encourage your own writing, as we believe that trying to write oneself leads to a better understanding of poetry and a greater facility in the use of language.

Every poem has therefore been chosen to illustrate a particular use of language and technique, and we hope this will ensure that there is something for everyone. Above all, we trust that reading these poems and writing your own will be both thought-provoking and enjoyable.

Sandy and Alan Brownjohn

Kit Wright

I started writing poems when I was about six, spurred on by my father who enjoyed writing them himself and it seemed to me then, and seems to me now, was very skilled at it. He published little and had no interest in doing so, but wrote because he liked it. And he encouraged me in the hope that I would derive the same pleasure from constructing those patterns of words that are poems.

I still think that this is the best reason for writing poetry, that one enjoys it. For me there is nothing more satisfying than making a poem, a dance without steps, a song without music, a drama in which the words are the actors. And the most exciting part of the process is the moment when the poem — quite suddenly, it always seems to me — starts taking shape, when the different elements in it begin to fuse together to make a new whole. When this magical break-through takes place seems completely unpredictable — assuming, of course, it takes place at all; like most poets, I've a Nelson's column of unfinished or abandoned manuscripts! But if it does, it might be right at the beginning with a couple of lines that seem to spark and crackle and light the way to an interesting village or land of the imagination, or it might be after hours and days of hacking through a dense jungle of words that won't give up their secret.

Of course, I didn't have any theories about writing poetry when I was six; I just made up poems from time to time and had fun. Thirty-four years later, I wonder what it is about a poem made as well as one can that gives such satisfaction. In one sense, I believe it's no different at all from the feeling of achievement a plumber gets from a neat and expert re-alignment of pipes, a motor mechanic from his skilled healing of an ailing engine, a computer game inventor from devising a nifty programme, a lawyer from drawing up a difficult contract, or a gardener from making things grow. In a more particular way, though, it's the music of poems that attracts me; not so much what the poem says, but the *tune* its meaning is set to.

Of course, one doesn't need to get too solemn about a poem that might not be much more than a joke in verse, and quite a few of my poems for younger (and older!) readers would fit that definition, but the idea of poetry as verbal tunes, as something very close to song, is central to every piece of verse I write. It's probably for this reason that so many of them have fairly strong rhythms and more often than not they're in rhyme.

In this anthology, my poem about the Down's Syndrome[1] child, 'Useful Person', has a repeated section like the refrain or chorus you find in most songs. 'The Song of the Whale', as the title suggests, is an attempt to find the words the whale might be singing to that sad, haunting music which you may have heard on a recording. And 'Mirror Poem' is really a little ballad the girl sings to her mirror at the

---

1   Down's Syndrome child, the correct medical term, is replacing the older term 'Mongol child'.

moment in the year when, according to an old story, she will see in it the man she's going to marry. (I've combined this with another superstition you probably know, the one that says breaking a mirror means seven years' bad luck.)

So these are songs of one kind and another. I may not have got them absolutely right, but they are as good as I could make them after working on them as hard as I could! I think 'Useful Person' might be a bit too long, for instance; and although the poem is meant to be conversational, there are places where I feel the language is a shade too flat. See what you think. Whatever the imperfections in my poems, though, I shall always be grateful to my father for introducing me to writing verse all those years ago — and I hope it's something you'll enjoy too.

The Song of The Whale

Heaving mountain in the sea,
Whale, I heard you
Grieving.

Great whale, crying for your life,
Crying for your kind, I knew
How we would use
Your dying:

Lipstick for our painted faces,
Polish for our shoes.

Tumbling mountain in the sea,
Whale, I heard you
Calling.

Bird-high notes, keening, soaring:
At their edge a tiny drum
Like a heartbeat.

We would make you
Dumb.

In the forest of the sea,
Whale, I heard you
Singing,

Singing to your own kind.
We'll never let you be.
Instead of life we choose

Lipstick for our painted faces,
Polish for our shoes.

Useful Person

We'd missed the train. Two hours to wait
On Lime Street Station, Liverpool,
With *not a single thing to do.*
The bar was shut and Dad was blue
And Mum was getting in a state
And everybody felt a fool.

Yes, we were very glum indeed.
Myself, I'd nothing new to read,
No sweets to eat, no game to play.
'I'm bored,' I said, and straight away,
Mum said what I knew she'd say:
'Go on, then, read a book, O.K.?'
'I've *read* them *both!*' 'That's no excuse.'

Dad sat sighing, '*What* a day. . .
This is precious little use.
I wish they'd open up that bar.'
They didn't, though. No way.

And everybody else was sitting
In that waiting-room and knitting,
Staring, scratching, yawning, smoking.
'All right, Dad?' 'You must be joking!
This is precious little use.
It's like a prison. Turn me loose!'

('Big fool, act your age!' Mum hisses.
'Sorry, missus.'
'Worse than him, you are,' said Mum.)

It was grim. It was glum.

And then the Mongol child came up,
Funny-faced:
Something in her body wrong,
Something in her mind
Misplaced:
Something in her eyes was strange:
What, or why, I couldn't tell:
But somehow she was beautiful
As well.

Anyway, she took us over!
'Hello, love,' said Dad. She said,
'*There*, sit *there*! and punched a spot
On the seat. The spot was what,
Almost, Mum was sitting on,
So Dad squeezed up, and head-to-head,
And crushed-up, hip-to-hip, they sat.
'What next, then?' 'Kiss!' 'Oh no, not that!'
Dad said, chuckling. '*Kiss!*'
                              They did!
I thought my Mum would flip her lid
With laughing. Then the Mongol child
Was filled with pleasure — she went wild,
Running round the tables, telling
Everyone to *kiss* and yelling
Out to everyone to sit
Where she said. They did, too. It
Was sudden happiness because
The Mongol child
Was what she was:
Bossy, happy, full of fun,
And just *determined* everyone
Should have a good time too! We knew
That's what we'd got to do.

Goodness me, she took us over!
All the passengers for Dover,
Wolverhampton, London, Crewe —
Everyone from everywhere
Began to share
Her point of view! The more they squeezed,
And laughed, and fooled about, the more
The Mongol child
Was pleased!

Dad had to kiss another Dad
('Watch it, lad!' 'You watch it, lad!'
'Stop: you're not my kind of bloke!')
Laugh? I thought my Mum would choke!

And so the time whirled by. The train
Whizzed us home again
And on the way I thought of her:
Precious little use is what
Things had been. Then she came
And things were not
The same!

She was precious, she was little,
She was useful too:
Made us speak when we were dumb,
Made us smile when we were blue,
Cheered us up when we were glum,
Lifted us when we were flat:
Who could be
More use than that?

Mongol child,
Funny-faced,
Something in your body wrong,
Something in your mind
Misplaced,
Something in your eyes, strange:
What, or why, I cannot tell:
I thought you were beautiful:

Useful, as well.

Mirror Poem

If I look within the mirror,
Deep inside its frozen tears,
Shall I see the man I'll marry
    Standing at my shoulder,
    Leaning down the years?

Shall I smile upon the mirror,
Shall my love look, smiling, back?
Midnight on midsummer's eve;
    What becomes of marriage
    If the glass should crack?

How to Treat the House-Plants

All she ever thinks about are house-plants.
She talks to them and tends them every day.
And she says, 'Don't hurt their feelings. Give them
Love. In all your dealings with them,
Treat them in a tender, *human* way.'

'Certainly, my dear,' he says. 'O.K.
Human, eh?'

But the house-plants do not seem to want to play.

They are stooping, they are drooping,
They are kneeling in their clay:
They are flaking, they are moulting,
Turning yellow, turning grey,
And they look . . . well, quite revolting
As they sigh, and fade away,

So after she has left the house he gets them
And he sets them in a line against the wall,
And I cannot say he cossets them or pets them —
No, he doesn't sympathise with them at all.
Is he tender? Is he human? Not a bit.
No, to each of them in turn he says: 'You *twit*!

You're a
     Rotten little skiver,
     Cost a fiver,
     Earn your keep!

You're a
    Dirty litttle drop-out!
    You're a cop-out!
    You're a creep!

You're a
    Mangy little whinger!
    You're a cringer!
    Son, it's true —

    I have justbin
    To the dustbin
    Where there's *better men than you*!
    Get that stem back!

    Pull your weight!

Stick your leaves out!

STAND UP STRAIGHT!

And, strange to say, the plants co-operate.
So when she comes back home and finds them glowing,
Green and healthy, every one a king,
She says, 'It's *tenderness* that gets them growing!
How strange, the change a little *love* can bring!'

'Oh yes,' he says. 'Not half. Right. Love's the thing.

Useful Person

'Useful Person' is one of a very few poems which treat subjects people usually 'shy away' from discussing. In this instance a Down's Syndrome child is the subject, and Kit Wright has made us think about our attitudes towards handicaps of all kinds. The obvious embarrassment and giggling of the 'normal' people in the poem eventually stops when they begin to relax, and take pleasure in the company of the child. Perhaps you have found this too? We ought to be honest with ourselves. Yes, we do feel awkward in the presence of anyone who is at all different (for whatever reason). And yes, some people act cruelly and callously in such situations, either out of fear or out of an insensitive inability to understand. But if we make the effort (and an effort it *can* be, to begin with) to relax and accept what is strange, we can frequently find our lives enriched by the experience. What experiences of this sort have you had yourself?

Mirror Poem

This short, two-stanza poem is based on the superstition that if a girl sits in front of a mirror on Midsummer Eve at midnight, she will see the reflection of the man she is going to marry. If she turns round, however, she will see no one, and the 'prophecy' will not come to pass. You will notice the song-like feel of the rhythm: the poem manages to capture the lilt of folk song and the air of simple folklore, including the suggestion of darker forces hinted at by the ending, which makes use of another superstition.

   How many superstitions can you list? Ask around your family, or consult friends from other parts of the country or from other countries altogether. You may like to base a poem of your own on one or more of these superstitions.

The Song of the Whale

Have you ever heard the so-called 'singing' of whales? There is a record of the 'Song of the Humpbacked Whale', and the sounds are among the most haunting it is possible to imagine. The words used by Kit Wright — *calling, singing, crying, grieving, keening* and *soaring* — are all descriptive of the sounds made by whales, and the simplicity of the poem's style, with its song-like refrain, communicates a strong note of protest in a very effective way.

   Poets, like other public figures — particularly those whose medium is words — might be said to have a duty to use their talents to comment on important public questions. Many do so, and in some countries the written word is considered so powerful that writers are often banned or imprisoned for their criticisms. Do you feel strongly about any matter — environmental, social, political — about which you could write a poem? If you feel something strongly, it is good to write about it. But be sure that you are marshalling your arguments thoughtfully and persuasively, and writing a genuine poem, not just a cry of protest.

How to Treat the House-Plants

Do plants respond to kind words and music as many people believe? Without taking sides on this particular question, it is possible to point out that there are many unusual, even peculiar, beliefs which can provide targets for satire.

In this case the image of the man treating the plants as raw, sloppy recruits in the army (or pupils at school?) and speaking to them in the role of sergeant-major (or head teacher?) is as funny as the wife who advocates the loving, caring approach. What do you think of the psychology involved? Do goading and challenging persuade people to respond more than kind words do?

It is worth commenting here on what Kit Wright says in his introduction about feeling that he may not always have completely succeeded with his poems, but has simply written them to the best of his ability. All poets, if they are honest, have mounds of discarded and unfinished poems which they cannot seem to get right or bring to a satisfactory conclusion. Even some of their published poems may show flaws; but they go on writing, and by continuing they improve. They become more and more self-critical, and less likely to be easily satisfied with what they have written. For the beginner it is helpful to realise and understand what experienced poets know very well: that it won't always come right at the first try (and sometimes not even at the tenth!), but that persistence will improve your skill in *any* kind of writing.

George Szirtes

Although for the last twelve years I have lived and worked in a small country town between London and Cambridge — and a very attractive town it is, too — I have always felt my real home was in a place more like the one in which I began my life, a city full of spectacular but rather tired-looking blocks of flats from the last century, somewhere in the middle of Europe.

My family arrived in this country as refugees from Hungary at the time of the revolution there in 1956. We came with nothing and lived in various parts of London an uneventful life, except that my mother was very ill and had to undergo an increasingly frequent number of operations. My brother and I learned to play musical instruments (he finished up as a musician), but I seemed likely to become some sort of scientist. That is until I turned seventeen, at which time I began reading and writing poetry, and painting pictures.

From the start I was lucky because a number of other science students in my school were also interested in poetry, and as we read things we liked we passed them on to each other. Since this wasn't exactly what we were supposed to be doing it felt encouragingly secret and rebellious. I knew from that time on that I wanted to be a poet. Or possibly an artist. Maybe both.

All the poems of mine here are, in their different ways, about danger. Two of them, 'The Cold Weather Cat' and 'Umbrellas', were written directly for my own children. My young daughter is very fond of cats and she noticed how in the winter their coats grow thicker and they look much fatter. They look so soft and puffed up that you could imagine them living a luxurious life as if by right. Yet often they are out at night in all weathers. This poem is about being comfortable and being exposed to wilder things, like the rain or a cutting wind. I wanted my cat, the Old Pariah, to be wise and kind, but with a growl at the back of his voice.

We tend to regard umbrellas as boring old articles, but there is an oddly bird-like feeling about them, especially when you shake them out. Many objects remind us of creatures, and when they do this they lose some of their familiarity and appear magical or even threatening. First the umbrella in my poem becomes a kind of sea anemone, then a crow with wet wings. Imagine a crow flying about in your hall leaving damp stains on the carpet. Lastly, umbrellas can be weapons. Not long ago a man was stabbed with a poisoned one. Really the poem is a bit of a joke, but a slightly sinister joke.

The 'Equilibrist' was someone I actually saw in a circus. It wasn't one of those top-flight circuses where everything runs like a machine — in fact, a lot of the acts went wrong or were simply not very good. (Secretly, I prefer this kind.) But there was one man who was quite brilliant — so brilliant that he came back three times, doing three different acts under three different names. In one of them he balanced a bewildering series of objects on his chin. I wanted to write a long, thin, clever and precariously-balanced poem to do him justice. This is the sort of poem it is positively fun to write. The danger here has become show-biz. And the poem is a piece of show-biz too.

The danger in 'A Small Girl Swinging' is quite real, though. Not that we can be certain of what it is. Do you know the feeling when you are the last one in a park or playground? And you are already late home and you know your parents will be worried about you? The girl in this poem is partly frightened by her own excitement as the swing leaps higher and higher. Eventually the swing goes so high it is almost as if she were off the planet altogether. Suddenly she realises that the people who have been pushing her are gone. Is that her own shadow on the ground?.

I wanted these poems to rhyme because songs rhyme and we tend to remember songs. And the things we remember seem to us, perhaps, the most true. Also I like playing ornate games with words. But this isn't always the best way and rhyme can be a bit of tyrant at times. Some poems want to rhyme, some don't. It is what the poems want to do that matters.

Equilibrist

A sword point is a sore point
In fact it's quite a bore,
A knee-joint is a neat joint
But hardly that much more,
A jaw bone is a raw bone
When it bears an awkward weight
And a scimitar's a limiter —
Of civilised debate —
But the feeling when one's kneeling
With a dagger at one's lip
And one yard above the poniard
A sword's fixed tip to tip!
One's talents are for balance
It's just as well to say
But crockery's a mockery
When set upon a tray
And the lot rests on a spot
Some six feet underneath
With sword and knife to threaten life —
You too would grit your teeth.
It's badder on a ladder
And may cause you some trouble
When the thing begins to swing
And the poniard starts to wobble.
A sword point is a sore point
As I have said before
And the groove does not improve
When you swoop across the floor —
But it must be fun when all is done
And everybody sees
You've been on before, and were what's more
THE MAN ON THE FLYING TRAPEZE.

A Small Girl Swinging

When first they pushed me
  I was very scared.
My tummy jiggled. I was
  Unprepared.

The second time was higher
  And my ears
Were cold with whisperings
  Of tiny fears.

The third time up was HIGH,
  My teeth on edge.
My heart leapt off the bedroom
  Windowledge.

The fourth time, oh, the fourth time
  It was mad.
My skirt flew off the world
  And I was glad.

No-one's pushing now,
  My ears are ringing.
Who'll see across the park
  A small girl swinging?

Who'll hear across the park
  Her mother calling,
And everywhere her shadows
  Rising, falling?

Umbrellas

What happens to old umbrellas?
I have seen them
take to air and ocean,
to attics and to cellars
with all the world between them.

One I know
lives fathomless below
at the very bottom of the sea-bed,
ribs transparent, beaded,
her skin a mouth in motion
wafting the dull billows of the ocean.

Another one I know
has turned into a crow
who when she flies
shakes out the rain
and leaves behind a small damp stain.

Don't mess with umbrellas.
They're weird, like awnings
of a homely size.
In the hall they serve as warnings
and poisoned ones are killers.

The Cold Weather Cat

Hear the Old Pariah purr,
nothing seems to bother her,
warm inside her coat of fur.

It's not easy to forgive her
being such an easy liver
while the winter makes us shiver.

O she's made of such warm stuff!
What if she can't take it off?
She seems equable enough

in her winter layer of fat.
Nothing remarkable in that.
So would I were I a cat.

My name is Old Pariah, I
give service keeping mice away.
I'm often treated like a toy.

Yes, I'm comfortable now
and warm enough, that I'll allow;
you do not hear my sad miaow,

you do not hear me scratch and screak
and yowl at night when I'm awake
and you are sleeping in the dark.

I know you'll say I'll domiciled
but last night when the wind was wild
it did not feel like that, my child.

The Cold Weather Cat

This poem is written in rhyming triplets: that is, each stanza consists of three lines which rhyme. Most of the rhymes here are full rhymes — *purr*, *her* and *fur* — which echo each other's sound exactly. But stanzas 3, 5 and 7 use half-rhymes — *I*, *away* and *toy* — which are similar in sound but not *exactly* the same. The poem has two voices speaking in it. The first four stanzas are the poet speaking, and the second four are given to the cat, Old Pariah. You might like to try writing a poem using the triplet form. Or you could try writing about an animal you know well (or know a lot about) — first with a description from your own point of view, and then a section written from the standpoint of the animal.

Umbrellas

Here is a poem about an everyday object seen in a new light. It is a good idea to try this as an exercise. Choose something so familiar to you that you normally do not even notice it — you take it completely for granted. See if you can find new images to describe it. Does it look like anything else? Do you know anything about any unusual uses that have been made of it? Stare at it, and see what pictures it conjures up.

Did you notice, by the way, that each of the lines in 'Umbrellas' rhymes with at least one other? There does not appear to be a definite pattern to the rhyme scheme, but when you look carefully you will notice the rhyming. One of the rhymes — *seen them*, *between them* — uses two words, and *umbrellas*, *killers* is a half-rhyme. Because the rhyme scheme is not regular in each stanza some freedom of manoeuvre becomes possible, thus avoiding one of the pitfalls of using rhyme: it can be *too noticeable* and detract from what the poem is saying.

Equilibrist

'Equilibrist' is all about balance, not only in its subject matter but in the wordplay George Szirtes uses with such pleasure throughout. The poem can be broken down into groups of four lines where the first and third, and the second and fourth, rhyme. Each alternate line is also made up of two phrases which rhyme, and balance:

> A *swordpoint* is a *sore point*

> And a *scimitar's* a *limiter*

You might like to make up sentences of your own that use this pattern of rhymes; it is good practice in hearing how words chime in with each other. As an example:

> It's a tall tree that's all free
> To grow up to the sky,
> And the rough bark makes a tough mark
> When you climb its branches, high.

You may find that when you have a couple of sentences a poem is beginning to take shape.

A Small Girl Swinging

In his introduction, George Szirtes tells us that there is a suggestion, a hint, of danger in this poem. Is the girl alone in the park? You might like to compare the poem with John Fuller's 'In a Railway Compartment' (page 115), and discuss how each poet has conveyed the subtle possibility of things not being as they seem, at the same time as describing what *can* be taken as a completely straightforward and innocent incident. The poem is in four-line stanzas (quatrains) where lines 2 and 4 rhyme (the pattern is a,b,c,b). Lines 2 and 4 are also shorter than the other two. The rhythm is predominantly iambic and it is noticeable that the poem could have been written out in another form. Lines 1 and 2 could have been one single line, and so could lines 3 and 4. This would have given us a poem in rhyming couplets and iambic pentameters (heroic couplets). But as it stands, the lines are no doubt a little more suggestive of a girl swinging to and fro.

Grace Nichols

My early childhood was spent in a small country village along the Guyana coast and my most treasured memory of it was of me, around the age of six, standing calf-deep in rippling brown water lit up by the sun, watching the moving shapes of fish below the surface. It was a remarkable place — water, water everywhere and sometimes, when it rained heavily, children came rowing to school in boats. When I was eight years old we moved to the city, Georgetown. It was me, my five sisters, one brother, my father (a headteacher), and my mother who was full of stories and verses she made, and who liked laughing.

I loved reading as a child (we had no television in Guyana) and sometimes I would sneak a torch into bed with me to finish off a book, after my father had switched off all the lights (which wasn't very good for my eyes).

After leaving high school I worked as, among other things, a primary school teacher, a clerk at a telephone company, a reporter with a daily national newspaper and a freelance journalist. When I came to Britain in 1977 I had already started writing stories for children and had a couple of poems published in a small magazine. I had also begun a novel.

The poem 'Candlefly' goes back to my childhood in the village when I had both a fascination and fear for the tiny neon insect which visited my bedroom ceiling from time to time, flickering in the dark. It was said by the older folk in the village that seeing a candlefly (also known as firefly) meant a stranger would visit. I used to be quite obsessed with who this stranger could be. Was this stranger by any chance Death? In a society where the supernatural is part of everyday life, where dreams do not go unheeded, my reaction to the candlefly was not that extraordinary.

'The Fat Black Woman Goes Shopping' is a humorous kind of poem from the cycle *The Fat Black Woman's Poems* — poems about a fat black woman, a persona I've created, who rejoices in herself while taking a satirical tongue-in-cheek view of the world. In the poem about shopping she's taking a dig at the fashion industry which tries to manipulate us, and dictate what we should wear. What size we should be. From my own observations, bigger people aren't really catered for in the average boutique. Why the fat black woman? I guess because the media bombard us with a fixed image of beauty — almost as if the whole world ought to be very slim and preferably blond.

The little poem 'Skin-teeth' begins with a Guyanese saying, 'Not every skin-teeth is a smile', meaning don't be deceived by appearances, not every smile is necessarily genuine. The saying in itself has sinister undertones and this feeling extends to the entire poem which comes from the section called 'The Sorcery' in *I is a long memoried woman*. I think the poem suggests the hidden power of the woman. She is plotting and planning even though to the eye she appears smiling and submissive, and it shows how an expression or even a word could give birth to a poem. In this poem the combination of 'skin' and 'teeth' is a very un-English one which illustrates the vividness and conciseness of Caribbean creole.

Candlefly

The candlefly
always came at night
blinking the ceiling
with its small searchlight

as a child I stared up
uneasily through the darkness
remembering the old folk saying

Candlefly means
a stranger will come
a stranger will visit

still I couldn't be comforted
the candlefly was both a magic
and a menace

a creature with a mission
a flickering stranger

                    not unlike death

The Fat Black Woman Goes Shopping

Shopping in London winter
is a real drag for the fat black woman
going from store to store
in search of accommodating clothes
and de weather so cold

Look at the frozen thin mannequins
fixing her with grin
and de pretty face salesgals
exchanging slimming glances
thinking she don't notice

Lord it's aggravating

Nothing soft and bright and billowing
to flow like breezy sunlight
when she walking

The fat black woman curses in Swahili/Yoruba
and nation language under her breathing
all this journeying and journeying

The fat black woman could only conclude
that when it come to fashion
the choice is lean

                Nothing much beyond size 14

Skin-teeth

Not every skin-teeth
is a smile 'Massa'

if you see me smiling
when you pass

if you see me bending
when you ask

Know that I smile
know that I bend

only the better
to rise and strike
again

Candlefly

How often superstitions have given rise to poems and stories! (Kit Wright's 'Mirror Poem', page 15, is an example.) This superstition from Guyana may remind you of one many older people will know: that a stranger will call on you if you see one tea-leaf floating on the tea in the cup. It is worth collecting superstitions, especially from other countries. They could supply ideas for poems, particularly if you can tell a story based on your own or someone else's actual experience. Have you ever heard of the belief that if you carefully peel an apple and watch the long strand of peel fall, it may form the initial letter of a boyfriend's or a girlfriend's name?

The Fat Black Woman Goes Shopping

Although the poem's subject is the fat black woman, it could apply to almost anyone who does not conform to the size of the so-called average person for whom fashion clothes seem to be made. Most of us when shopping find we are too tall/short, too fat/thin, too small in one part of our body and too large in another, for the standard measurements. Women with shoe sizes less than 4 and more than 7 certainly know this problem.

The poem shows the fat black woman's thoughts on what she would prefer to wear, and also reveals that she is aware of other people's reactions to her. It is no wonder she curses, although she seems to accept matters fairly philosophically; as Grace Nichols says, this is a humorous poem. Its form is: two stanzas of five lines, followed by one separate three-word line, followed by two stanzas of three lines, and then one last line. The last two lines rhyme, to round off the poem with almost a joking 'punch-line'. There is a strong rhythmic quality to the poem, as there is in all the poems in this section.

When writing your own poems, remember that there are many different techniques and forms you can employ. You may choose to use rhyme, or a traditional, regular rhythm — or you may write in lines which echo your own natural speech rhythms. Everybody has his or her own natural rhythmic feel, and by using your own speech rhythms you may find it easier to express what you have to say. Why not try the experiment of tape-recording yourself in conversation with others, and then analysing the sound of your speech? Note the beats where your voice stresses words, and the pauses you make. Then, when you write, try using these same patterns. You should find it comes naturally, and may help your thoughts (and words) to flow.

Skin-teeth

There is a strong rhythm here, too, and the poem makes use of half-rhymes: 'pass' and 'ask', 'band' and 'again'. As Grace Nichols explains, this poem arises out of a saying. Sayings can be another source of ideas for poems, another useful collection to make. Again, sayings from countries other than your own can often spark off a train of thought, partly because they are new and fresh-sounding. But even sayings which you may frequently use yourself can take on a new life when looked at on their own. 'People in glass houses should not throw stones.' 'Out of the frying pan into the fire.' 'Building castles in the air.' 'All fingers and thumbs.' These are all sayings and proverbs which could be explored as subjects for poems. Can you think of others?

Edwin Morgan

I was born in Scotland, in the city of Glasgow, and I have always
made my home there, though I have travelled fairly widely in different parts of the world. During the Second World War, I served as a
private in the Royal Army Medical Corps, in Egypt, Palestine, and
Lebanon. My main work has been teaching English literature to university students, but I have also done a good deal of broadcasting and
book-reviewing, and I have written the librettos for several operas
and other kinds of musical performance.

I began writing at school, when I was about ten or eleven, and produced not only poems but lots of long stories and essays, many of them very imaginative. I loved words — used to collect lists of words that appealed to me. And the sounds of words, as well as their meaning, made a strong impact. My poetry is of different kinds. Because of my city background — and I like cities of all sorts and sizes! — I have many poems of city life, often realistic, down-to-earth, hard-hitting, sometimes humorous, and generally about Glasgow. But the fascination of words themselves, and the interest I have mentioned in music and sound-effects, also led me to a more experimental kind of poetry, a poetry where the voice really has to be heard. Even if this poetry is printed in books, it is asking and tempting you to speak it aloud, to try out its sound, to see whether it means more when you hear it than when you read it silently. Some of these poems could be called 'performance poems', and in a sense there is nothing new about this, since from the earliest times poets have recited their work in public and been rewarded and applauded (or no doubt sometimes booed!) by a live audience.

'The Loch Ness Monster's Song' is an example of a performance piece. It absolutely demands to be read aloud, and the way the lines are set out, the spelling, the punctuation are all devised — even if it might not seem so at first glance: — to help the performance. It needs a bit of practice, but it can be done, and although I have recorded the poem myself on tape, I would not want to say that there is only one way of reading it. Anyone can have a go — and enjoy it. Whether the Loch Ness Monster really exists or not — there is no clinching evidence — I imagine the creature coming to the surface of the water, looking round at the world, expressing his or her views, and sinking back into the loch at the end. I wanted to have a mixture of the bubbling, gurgling, plopping sounds of water and the deep gruff throaty sounds that a large aquatic monster might be expected to make. How much meaning comes through the sounds? A little? I leave that to you!

One of my long-standing interests has been science-fiction. Even at school I remember devouring the wild tales in magazines like *Amazing Stories* and also reading the books of Jules Verne and H.G. Wells. I enjoy writing science-fiction poems, and try to give them some 'point', so that they are not merely fantastic. In 'The First Men on Mercury', I imagine the first successful Earth expedition to the planet Mercury, and an attempt at conversation between the leader of the expedition and the first Mercurian who comes up to see what has happened. Again, to get the full effect of this poem, you ought to try reading it aloud, or of course it can be done with two voices. And the poem is not just about communication — I am sure you will find other themes and meanings. Earthman conquers the universe — or does he?

'Off Course' is one of a number of 'spacepoems' I wrote about the early rockets which were sent up by Russia and America. This one is about a disastrous moon voyage (imaginary, but related to some of the actual disasters which did take place) where the rocket goes off course and explodes, all the men inside being killed. The moment of crisis is shown by the indenting of the last seven lines: the poem itself is literally driven 'off course'. The scrambled images of the last part are meant to act out the chaotic scene of the rocket breaking up.

I suppose 'Flakes', too, is about voyages to the moon, but it is a sort of nursery rhyme as well. The unexpected images, and the jumps in the story, are like some of the effects in folk-poetry, and I liked the idea of using such techniques to talk about something as modern and scientific as a moon walk.

The First Men on Mercury

— We come in peace from the third planet.
Would you take us to your leader?

— Bawr stretter! Bawr. Bawr. Stretterhawl?

— This is a little plastic model
of the solar system, with working parts.
You are here and we are there and we
are now here with you, is this clear?

— Gawl horrop. Bawr. Abawrhannahanna!

— Where we come from is blue and white
with brown, you see we call the brown
here 'land', the blue is 'sea', and the white
is 'clouds' over land and sea, we live
on the surface of the brown land,
all round is sea and clouds. We are 'men'.
Men come —

— Glawp men! Gawrbenner menko. Menhawl?

— Men come in peace from the third planet
which we call 'earth'. We are earthmen.
Take us earthmen to your leader.

— Thmen? Thmen? Bawr. Bawrhossop.
Yuleeda tan hanna. Harrabost yuleeda.

— I am the yuleeda. You see my hands,
we carry no benner, we come in peace.
The spaceways are all stretterhawn.

— Glawn peacemen all horrabhanna tantko!
Tan come at'mstrossop. Glawp yuleeda!

— Atoms are peacegawl in our harraban.
Menbat worrabost from tan hannahanna.

— You men we know bawrhossoptant. Bawr.
We know yuleeda. Go strawg backspetter quick.

— We cantantabawr, tantingko backspetter now!

— Banghapper now! Yes, third planet back.
Yuleeda will go back blue, white, brown
nowhanna! There is no more talk.

— Gawl han fasthapper?

— No. You must go back to your planet.
Go back in peace, take what you have gained
but quickly.

— Stretterworra gawl, gawl . . .

— Of course, but nothing is ever the same,
now is it? You'll remember Mercury.

The Loch Ness Monster's Song

Sssnnnwhufffll?
Hnwhuffl hhnnwfl hnfl hfl?
Gdroblboblhobngbl gbl gl g g g g glbgl.
Drublhaflablhaflubhafgabhaflhafl fl fl—
gm grawwwww grf grawf awfgm graw gm.
Hovoplodok-doplodovok-plovodokot-doplodokosh?
Splgraw fok fok splgrafhatchgabrlgabrl fok splfok!
Zgra kra gka fok!
Grof grawff gahf?
Gombl mbl bl—
blm plm,
blm plm,
blm plm,
blp.

Spacepoem 3: Off Course

the golden flood   the weightless seat
the cabin song   the pitch black
the growing beard   the floating crumb
the shining rendezvous   the orbit wisecrack
the hot spacesuit   the smuggled mouth-organ
the imaginary somersault   the visionary sunrise
the turning continents   the space debris
the golden lifeline   the space walk
the crawling deltas   the camera moon
the pitch velvet   the rough sleep
the crackling headphone   the space silence
the turning earth   the lifeline continents
the cabin sunrise   the hot flood
the shining spacesuit   the growing moon
  the crackling somersault   the smuggled orbit
  the rough moon   the visionary rendezvous
  the weightless headphone   the cabin debris
  the floating lifeline   the pitch sleep
  the crawling camera   the turning silence
  the space crumb   the crackling beard
  the orbit mouth-organ   the floating song

Flakes

this is the blizzard
that ate the robin
that hopped on the dish
that filled with snow

this is the corrie
that cooked the blizzard
that ate the robin
that hopped on the dish

this is the cloud
that lit the corrie
that cooked the blizzard
that ate the robin

this is the moon
that crazed the cloud
that lit the corrie
that cooked the blizzard

this is the boots
that tramped the moon
that crazed the cloud
and filled with snow

The First Men on Mercury

This is a poem to read out loud, with perhaps two voices, one for the earthmen and another for the men of Mercury. The way the language of one subtly changes into the language of the other is very cleverly and amusingly achieved. The poem makes a good performance piece. It is included here purely for enjoyment, and to show that there are always new possibilities for the creative mind to delight in — playing with the sounds of language as well as the meaning.

The Loch Ness Monster's Song

Again this is a sound poem which cries out to be read aloud. As you can see, it uses invented 'words', and at first glance may appear impossible to speak. But if you sound out the letters you will begin to hear the patterns and reasons behind the poem. Certain sounds seem to echo those of a boat going across the loch, and many others seem to have the muffled or hollow quality of sounds heard from under water. The whole poem has been very carefully worked out — not just thrown down at random.

It is difficult to compete with so successful a poem as this, but you may like to write your own as an exercise in trying to reproduce natural sounds in made-up words. You may have come across some of the words that certain bird identification books use for describing birdsong — 'peewit' is one of these. Choose a creature (for example, an insect), or even an object or a machine that makes a noise, and try to invent words which resemble the sounds it makes. It might be a good idea to imagine what the creature is *actually* saying, so as to incorporate the right 'tone of voice' in your poem.

Spacepoem 3: Off Course

'Spacepoem 3: Off Course' is a list poem — in its own way. It consists of lists of phrases, two to a line. But it also has some similarities to John Mole's poem 'Song of the Diplomat' (page 107), in that certain words change places as the poem progresses. As used here, this device has the effect of showing us what happens when the spacecraft goes off course. As the words swap places, so things begin to go wrong, and by the end we must assume that the spaceship itself has come to an end. Such phrases as 'the floating lifeline', 'the turning silence' and 'the orbit mouth-organ' suggest catastrophe.

You might take a subject with a story line to write about in this way. Some possibilities: a ship that hits a rock and sinks; a cat playing with string and becoming thoroughly entangled in it; two people in a supermarket, pushing trolleys of food, have a collision and the food ends up in a mess on the floor. The second two ideas could be used to describe the muddle at the end in a thorough mix-up of words and phrases.

Flakes

'Flakes' is the poem that came from the rhyme that described the characters that lived in the house that Jack built! The basic pattern is taken from the old nursery rhyme, but is changed; new lines are added and old lines are dropped. There are numerous nursery rhymes which we learned and enjoyed when very young, and then discarded as we grew up and thought ourselves too old for them. But they are worth trying to remember, as they can be a useful source of ideas for poems. As with 'Leaves', by Ted Hughes (page 98), you can take an old rhyme and use its pattern to give you a form for something new. You can adapt the patterns to suit your subject-matter, but you will find that nursery rhymes, and also traditional songs, are strong on rhythm (and rhyme) and can be very satisfying to imitate.

Vernon Scannell

I was born in 1922, four years after the First World War ended, and my early childhood was spent in the shadows cast by that terrible and wasteful struggle. My father fought in the trenches and he was a young infantry sergeant when he married my mother. He often talked about his experiences in the Army and these tales, together with the photographs of the landscapes of war (and machinery) in the popular histories that were published in weekly magazines, became an important part of my imaginative development. The songs, martial or sentimental, of the war years were still sung round the piano or played on the wind-up gramophones and they too formed another strand in the fabric of my private world at that time. As I grew into my early teens I began to read the stories and poems written by men who had fought — and in some cases died — in the 1914–18 War with Germany and, even now, I find myself still fascinated and moved by the events, the songs, the suffering, glory and horror of a time that has gone forever. When I myself became a soldier in World War II, I felt that this war was somehow less dramatic, less tragic, less heroic than my father's war. The war against Hitler was, in my view, what Christians call a 'just war'. There was no other way to deal with Nazi aggression than to fight against it. Yet the spirit of the Second World War was bleak, resigned, dour. Along with the squalor, boredom, fear and deprecation, the compensatory virtues of comradeship, courage and self-sacrifice, were displayed. But, to me, these seemed smaller, less resonant than the vast, humbling anguish, nobility and sadness of World War I.

'Uncle Edward's Affliction' is intended to express something of my admiration for the generation which fought in the filth and carnage of the trenches in the 1914–18 war. It is not factual in that I do not possess an Uncle Edward who is colour-blind. But I once met a young husband and wife who did have an uncle — I don't know his name — and he was, they told me, 'an irritating old bore'. When I asked why he was so boring and irritating they said, 'He's colour-blind and he will go on about the First World War. He's obsessed by it. Always talking about being wounded on the Somme.' Well, as you will see by the poem, my sympathy was entirely with the old man.

In 'Dead Dog' I do what quite a few poets do and that is go back to an incident in my very early childhood which I remember vividly and use the poem as a kind of instrument of excavation to dig into the past and find out why this particular event has haunted my memory every since. The poem — as perhaps most poems do — asks questions, in this case about human attitudes to the fact of death, but it does not supply answers. It is the reader who might do that by thinking and feeling about the experience described, and perhaps relating it to some similar (experience) of his or her own. 'A Case of Murder' is *not* about my own childhood, but it could be. It takes the story of a boy (he was in fact the son of an acquaintance of mine) who, half accidentally and half on purpose, kills the family cat. Again it is for the reader to decide what is meant by the gigantic cat that bursts out of the cupboard to avenge itself on the boy. An important general point about the way in which poetry works: to me this poem is about cruelty, violence, temptation, guilt and repression. None of these words appears in the poem. In fact there are almost no abstract words at all. The ideas are conveyed through actual *objects* and *actions*. Most poetry, particularly of the twentieth century, does not *talk about* things; it makes them happen.

Finally, 'Incendiary' is based on an actual happening. The boy who set fire to the haystacks and barn was an inmate of a home for maladjusted children in Kent. I knew one of the people who looked after these children, and he told me that this boy, who was illegitimate, had come, via the juvenile courts, from an appalling foster-home where he had been ill-treated and had never been shown a flicker of normal human affection. The poem suggests that, because he was emotionally frozen, that is, had never received the warmth of parental love, he created a great blaze as a kind of symbolic compensation for this lack. But of course you the reader are perfectly entitled to disagree with this suggestion and take a quite different view of his behaviour.

Uncle Edward's Affliction

Uncle Edward was colour-blind;
We grew accustomed to the fact.
When he asked someone to hand him
The green book from the window-seat
And we observed its bright red cover
Either apathy or tact
Stifled comment. We passed it over.
Much later, I began to wonder
What curious world he wandered in,
Down streets where pea-green pillar-boxes
Grinned at a fire engine as green;
How Uncle Edward's sky at dawn
And sunset flooded marshy green.
Did he ken John Peel with his coat so green
And Robin Hood in Lincoln red?
On country walks avoid being stung
By nettles hot as a witch's tongue?
What meals he savoured with his eyes:
Green strawberries and fresh red peas,
Green beef and greener burgundy.
All unscientific, so it seems:
His world was not at all like that,
So those who claim to know have said.
Yet, I believe, in war-smashed France
He must have crawled from neutral mud
To lie in pastures dark and red
And seen, appalled, on every blade
The rain of innocent green blood.

A Case of Murder

They should not have left him there alone,
Alone that is except for the cat.
He was only nine, not old enough
To be left alone in a basement flat,
Alone, that is, except for the cat.
A dog would have been a different thing,
A big gruff dog with slashing jaws,
But a cat with round eyes mad as gold,
Plump as a cushion with tucked-in paws —
Better have left him with a fair-sized rat!
But what they did was leave him with a cat.
He hated that cat; he watched it sit,
A buzzing machine of soft black stuff,
He sat and watched and he hated it,
Snug in its fur, hot blood in a muff,
And its mad gold stare and the way it sat
Crooning dark warmth: he loathed all that.
So he took Daddy's stick and he hit the cat.
Then quick as a sudden crack in glass
It hissed, black flash, to a hiding place
In the dust and dark beneath the couch,
And he followed the grin on his new-made face,
A wide-eyed, frightened snarl of a grin,
And he took the stick and he thrust it in,
Hard and quick in the furry dark.
The black fur squealed and he felt his skin
Prickle with sparks of dry delight.
Then the cat again came into sight,
Shot for the door that wasn't quite shut,
But the boy, quick too, slammed fast the door:
The cat, half-through, was cracked like a nut
And the soft black thud was dumped on the floor.
Then the boy was suddenly terrified
And he bit his knuckles and cried and cried;
But he had to do something with the dead thing there.

His eyes squeezed beads of salty prayer
But the wound of fear gaped wide and raw;
He dared not touch the thing with his hands
So he fetched a spade and shovelled it
And dumped the load of heavy fur
In the spidery cupboard under the stair
Where it's been for years, and though it died
It's grown in that cupboard and its hot low purr
Grows slowly louder year by year:
There'll not be a corner for the boy to hide
When the cupboard swells and all sides split
And the huge black cat pads out of it.

Dead Dog

One day I found a lost dog in the street.
The hairs about its grin were spiked with blood,
And it lay still as stone. It must have been
A little dog, for though I only stood
Nine inches for each one of my four years
I picked it up and took it home. My mother
Squealed, and later father spaded out
A bed and tucked my mongrel down in mud.

I can't remember any feeling but
A moderate pity, cool not swollen-eyed;
Almost a godlike feeling now it seems.
My lump of dog was ordinary as bread.
I have no recollection of the school
Where I was taught my terror of the dead.

Incendiary

That one small boy with a face like pallid cheese
And burnt-out little eyes could make a blaze
As brazen, fierce and huge, as red and gold
And zany yellow as the one that spoiled
Three thousand guineas' worth of property
And crops at Godwin's Farm on Saturday
Is frightening — as fact and metaphor:
An ordinary match intended for
The lighting of a pipe or kitchen fire
Misused may set a whole menagerie
Of flame-fanged tigers roaring hungrily.
And frightening, too, that one small boy should set
The sky on fire and choke the stars to heat
Such skinny limbs and such a little heart
Which would have been content with one warm kiss
Had there been anyone to offer this.

Uncle Edward's Affliction

Colour-blindness normally takes the form of being 'red-green blind.'
You are unable to distinguish between the two colours. What Vernon
Scannell has done is to use 'poetic licence' and make play with the
common belief that you see red as green and *vice versa*. The images this
conjures up are quite startling, rather like a surrealist painting: a
green sunset, green strawberries, and red peas. But Uncle Edward's
affliction might be seen more as the memory of his appalling experiences in the First World War, memories which haunted him for the
rest of his life. A fine ending to the poem brings together the two
'afflictions'. The word 'green' in the last line carries with it the sense
of 'innocent', 'young' and 'inexperienced', thus highlighting the
plight of the thousands of very young soldiers who lost their lives in
that dreadful war. It reminds us, too, that other poets, participants in
that war, referred to the fields of bright red poppies which seemed to
symbolise the blood spilt. If you would like to read some of their work,
try looking at poems by Wilfred Owen, Siegfried Sassoon, Isaac
Rosenberg and others, in the *Penguin Book of First World War Poetry*.
Vernon Scannell has written poems about the Second World War,
and one of his finest is 'Walking Wounded', which would give you
further insight into his feelings on this subject.

Dead Dog

This poem is written in the iambic rhythm (in this case, iambic pentameters) which Vernon Scannell often uses. Notice how he runs lines
on so that when you read the poem for the sense (not simply line by
line), the rhythm is still felt, and holds the poem together — but is not
monotonous or obtrusive.

   Most of us will at some time have dug graves for dead animals,
perhaps pets. Do you have a memory of such an experience, about
which you could write? Remember it is the *details* which will convey
the experience, and your feelings about it, to others. Notice, in 'Dead
Dog', the sharp and original use of language in phrases like 'The hairs
about *its grin*' and 'later father *spaded out*/A bed'.

A Case of Murder

This tells the story of the death of a cat at the hands of a small boy; it is quite shocking and disconcerting. The poem rhymes throughout, sometimes in alternate lines, sometimes in pairs of lines (couplets) — the rhyme seems to add to the horror. Yet when you examine the ending, the poem seems to gain a wider meaning, or becomes something other than a mere story. Does the growing cat represent the man's conscience? Does the tale of the cat's murder stand for something else altogether? Did the boy really kill the cat? The descriptions of the cat make it almost larger than life: 'round eyes mad as gold,/Plump as a cushion with tucked-in paws', 'A buzzing machine of soft black stuff,/Snug in its fur, hot blood in a muff'. The poem expresses the terror of animal forces unleashed, through such lines as 'And he followed the grin of his new-made face,/A wide-eyed, frightened snarl of a grin'. It is clear that although such actions are recognised as part of human nature by the poet, they are, nevertheless, not condoned or admired. Aggression of this kind is most often inflicted on a weaker victim. You may like to discuss examples from world news: political prisoners, great powers or large organisations persecuting an individual or a minority. Or you may have examples closer to home. Have you ever imagined anything similar to the story of this poem?

Incendiary

This is another poem written in iambic pentameters and employing rhyme. As Vernon Scannell indicates, it tells of an act of arson which seemed to symbolise a cry for help from a boy who had been deprived of warmth, love and family. Often crimes of this seemingly senseless nature are committed by people whose minds are for some reason disturbed. This does not necessarily make it any easier for society to know how to help them, and there is a natural feeling that crime must be punished or corrected in some way. But what do you think? What would your reaction be if the property of someone in another town was burnt down? What if it were yours? Would you take a short-term or long-term view? Would you be right?

Alan Brownjohn

I come from four generations of Londoners, on both sides of my family. I went to school in London, grew up there, and have always worked there, as a teacher, lecturer, writer, broadcaster, though I am strongly drawn to other parts of the country like Norfolk. The only gaps in this London life were my years as an 'evacuee' in Cornwall during the Second World War, and my three years as a student at Oxford.

University was the place where writing really started for me. At university I learnt the pleasure and value of being among other students who themselves wanted to write, and who were always eager to see and criticise my own efforts. But I am certain I would have been a writer whatever I had done after schooldays. I had been writing poems and stories in a secret notebook from thirteen onwards (these are now lost), and keeping a full private diary from the same age (I still have some volumes of that.)

Secrecy, privacy? Not all poetry is concerned with very private feelings of joy, or yearning, or puzzlement, of fear — but some is. Some of mine certainly is. 'Grey Ground' is about those moments when you experience a fear you cannot explain. You need not be afraid of a room, or a place, or the dark, yet you *are* afraid. I visited the site of a deserted tin mine when I lived in Cornwall. The shaft itself was very dangerous. But the nearby ground was safe enough. So why did it seem as if a voice in the air (and in the trees, and in the echoes made by pebbles dropped down the mine) was warning me? And why did the feeling return when I went back thirty years later? Such strange feelings can be very powerful, and it is not surprising that people invent superstitious or supernatural explanations for them.

Sometimes poets are asked to supply poems on particular subjects for books or magazines. Asked to write about crabs — of which I knew next to nothing! — I hunted desperately for information in an encyclopaedia, and began to write out the facts I was learning in short, rhyming verses. Soon it seemed to me that these were not going to be enough. I decided to have two 'stories' happening at once, and wrote the two-line sections, describing one very old crab walking on a beach, to be placed between the four-liners. The longer lines are serious, the rhyming sections are intended to be comic in a slightly sinister way. 'Crabwise' seemed a suitable title.

It is quite allowed — and quite possible — to 'find' poems in places where you would not think poetry existed. I took six sums from an old arithmetic book, and set them out as verses; then found a seventh 'verse' in the introduction to the book — and I had a poem about things regarded as 'Common Sense' around 1917: gardeners were underpaid, milkmen diluted the milk, the country had thousands of paupers, armies could lose thousands of men and be expected to go on fighting. There is a bitter tone in the poem as well as a humorous one.

A few years ago, spending a fortnight in February in the Yorkshire hills, I could understand what bitter winter weather is like for people who live permanently in very cold places. Each day that February the thaw would *appear* to be coming when the sun shone overhead. And yet, at the same time, the frost was creeping out again under our feet. 'Heptonstall February' is about a cold winter month in a place where the streams were frozen (waterfalls became icicles) and the air was bitter and treacherous. I wanted the cold to come to the window of the room where we all sat warm indoors, and learn how to thaw from the warmth of the people!

'Inheritors'? It's simply a mysterious little picture which has no particular explanation. There are clues, but no answer. What — or who? — is the owl? Has it some connection with the sinister figures in the scarlet room? Are they suspicious of each other, and if so, why? The title suggests they have inherited the house. By foul means? And what will happen next? It is anyone's guess. Including mine.

Grey Ground

In the Cornwall wind
I stood with the mine-shaft behind me.
Something said, a toneless kind-of-voice said, 'Don't
Walk on that ground.'

The ground was plain mud and stones, a grey stretch, safe.
But, 'Don't walk on that ground.'
I had flung and heard the pebbles in the dark shaft
Fenced off under the brick stack, black.
Was the grey ground not safe?

The wind worked at the firs' tops,
It had that whisper, 'Don't walk on
That ground.' The pebbles in the shaft
Clanged, and hit echoes. The echoes touched out
Echoes. The echoes said, 'Don't walk on that
Ground.'

The death-shaft gulped and trapped the echoes of the pebbles.
The ground was mud and stones, is mud and stones,
A grey stretch, not fenced off now, thirty years
Safe, still. People have walked on it,
Thirty years.
I did not walk on it when I was ten.

I stand here, thirty years after, in the Cornwall wind
A man, looking at the grey ground. The firs' tops
Work and whisper.
The day is a clearer day, the sea visible,

The sun is out. A woman touches my arm,
We are standing with the mine-shaft behind us swallowing
Echoes of thirty years ago, of a minute ago,
Pebbles we have both thrown, smiling.

Something says, a toneless kind-of voice says
'Don't walk on that ground.'

Crabwise

Sea-crabs live in
And near the sea,
Land-crabs go back
Occasionally.

After these many months the old crab was out of the water,
And into the full, blank air and wanting the sun.

A crab has a very strange
Sideways walk
And eyes placed on
A retracting stalk.

Wide sheets of wet light covered the level beach
As he came fumbling and peering over the gnarled sand.

Two kinds of bodies
For crabs there are:
The oval and
The triangular.

His ten legs carried his squat bulk grave-
ly and slowly like a burden all too sad to keep long.

A little crab only
Really begins
To be adult when he's
Cast five skins.

This was the last stroll of years out of the bitter flow and
Hard swirl of the winter water, dragging from pool to clear
pool.

A crab's feet are not
All the same, because
Some are for walking
And some have jaws.

His old mouths muttered on the windy silence as he walked.
In his funny clumsiness and misery he was man-like.

Common Sense

An argricultural labourer, who has
A wife and four children, receives 20s a week.
¾ buys food, and the members of the family
Have three meals a day.
How much is that per person per meal?
> *– From Pitman's Common Sense Arithmetic, 1917*

A gardener, paid 24s a week, is
Fined 1/3 if he comes to work late.
At the end of 26 weeks, he receives
£30.5.3. How
Often was he late?
> *– From Pitman's Common Sense Arithmetic, 1917*

A milk dealer buys milk at 3d. a quart. He
Dilutes it with 3% water and sells
124 gallons of the mixture at
4d. per quart. How much of his profit is made by
Adulterating the milk?
> *– From Pitman's Common Sense Arithmetic, 1917*

The table printed below gives the number
Of paupers in the United Kingdom, and
The total cost of poor relief.
Find the average number
Of paupers per ten thousand people.
> *– From Pitman's Common Sense Arithmetic, 1917*

An army had to march to the relief of
A besieged town, 500 miles away, which
Had telegraphed that it could hold out for 18 days.
The army made forced marches at the rate of 18
Miles a day. Would it be there in time?
> *– From Pitman's Common Sense Arithmetic, 1917*

Out of an army of 28,000 men,
15% were
Killed, 25% were
Wounded. Calculate
How many men there were left to fight.
    — From Pitman's Common Sense Arithmetic, 1917

These sums are offered to
That host of young people in our Elementary Schools, who
Are so ardently desirous of setting
Foot upon the first rung of the
Educational ladder . . .
    — From Pitman's Common Sense Arithmetic, 1917

Heptonstall February

Today the moors unclench and clench
On a gift of warmth, the snow
Draws back one softened inch, but frost holds firm.
In our mid-afternoon new ice already
Glints in the sun's very eye. A camera eye
Would trace the loosened stream, and stop
On a rigid freeze: where suddenly grey
Spires, that were a waterfall, stab down
At the shrunken torrent.
                    None of these days
Will release themselves, the land
Not gentle into sympathy. This cold
Is well ignored by those who wait indoors
Inside their coloured windows, watching
The month increase and the land not change:
Let it come to the light and listen.

Inheritors

The snow is at the same time as the owl;
When it drops to the sill, the wings close,

First question: *Why should the owl*
Fly down each night to peer at our painted room?

Softly the snow-dots tumble from its back
As it stands on still claws and looks in,

Second question: *Why does the owl*
Stare in so long at our wine and velvet chairs?

Away from its nest, old feathers, suspicious gaze,
Away if you walk near the window, but always back,

Third question: *If one of us has summoned it,*
Which?

— And so we sit, four men in a shared house,
In a particularly scarlet room,
Not easy as we snow down cards, four
After four on the shining table-top;

Not easy as our fingers claw them in;
Wondering what is meant by these visits
From two old interested eyes, not easy
Wondering also which of us might know.

Grey Ground

The poem is concerned with a real experience. It has a slightly mysterious air. The use of repetition — the repeated instruction *Don't walk
on that ground* — helps to create an atmosphere of foreboding. The
way the words seem to emerge from everything in the surrounding
scene, the fir trees, the mine (as well as the insistent inner voice), must
be a familiar experience to all of us. Can you think of an occasion
when you did not do something because a feeling inside you led you to
think it might be dangerous, though you could not say why? It might
be a good subject for a poem of your own. If it *is* your own experience,
see if you can find ways of communicating to others the thoughts
which went through your own mind.

Crabwise

'Crabwise' has some similarity to 'Common Sense' (see below)
inasmuch as the four-line stanzas are constructed out of facts looked
up in an encyclopaedia. It is not a found poem, but it almost fits into
that category. The facts about crabs are arranged in quatrains in
which lines 2 and 4 rhyme. There is a jaunty, rather humorous tone,
almost as if the poet wanted to find a way to help him remember the
details. Rhymes make facts more memorable and often occur in
mnemonics — aids to memory like the well-known jingle 'Thirty
days hath September,/April, June and November'. In 'Crabwise',
the more serious-sounding alternate two-line stanzas use the details
about crabs to write about one real crab. They contrast effectively
with the lighter four-line sections.

   Looking up some facts in a reference book might provide you with
one way of starting a poem. See if the imaginative ideas will flow from
the supply of factual detail which the book gives. A successful use of
accurate facts can give a poem body and interest; poetry need not be
entirely a matter of imaginary scenes or events.

Common Sense

This is an example of a Found Poem. By this we mean that the poet
has found the words in some other printed material and recognised
the possibility of setting them out in lines to make a poem. They are
put down just as they are, without any rewriting, because they are
strange, or unusual, or interesting enough to stand on their own. You
are very lucky if you find just the right sort of material, although
someone once set out as a poem a small section of the entries from a
telephone directory under the name Smith. The result was a wide

variety of Smiths, with very different addresses, presenting a cross-section of society. 'Common Sense' is a series of sums from a 1917 arithmetic book, and it too succeeds in presenting a picture of society as it was then. I wonder whether present-day maths books would give a similar picture of how we live now? You might like to search for a 'found poem.' Possible sources might be encyclopaedia entries, cereal packets, lonely hearts columns (some poets have used this idea but written their own entries) and newspaper reports.

Heptonstall February

This short poem describes in some detail a particular scene and the effect of the weather on it; it is set in one definite landscape and time of year. In June the same place would present a very different picture. A seashore in December would hardly be the same place that it was in August. Try choosing a place you know well, and describe it as it is in a particular month. You will have to pay close attention to detail and find ways of describing the scene which are new and exciting, so as to provide a vivid picture in your poem.

Inheritors

As the poet suggests in his introduction, there is a mystery here. The use of questions helps to plant a suspicion. And then the use of the owl and snow imagery throughout the poem helps to create an atmosphere of unease: 'Not easy as we snow down cards', 'Not easy as our fingers claw them in'. Notice the contrast in colour of the white snow with the scarlet room and its wine-coloured chairs, and the echo of softness in the snowflakes, the owl's feathers and the velvet chairs. It is by using such techniques that you can subtly portray a scene in such a way as to give it mystery.

Pete Morgan

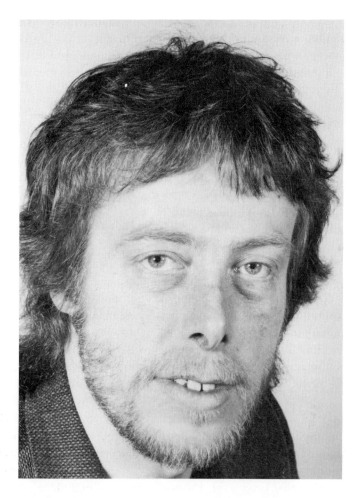

I was born in Leigh, in Lancashire, and spent my childhood there. In those days Leigh was a grubby industrial town and the only thing I liked about the place was the Rugby League team.

Every Saturday I caught the bus to Kirkhall Lane, paid my 1s. 9d, and stood in the cold to watch the likes of Jimmy Ledgard and Charlie Pawsey take on the might of Wigan or Warrington. Those men were heroes.

Apart from the joy of Saturdays I spent most of my time wishing I was somewhere elsc, anywhere apart from Leigh.

My first interest in poetry was probably a form of escapism. If I lifted my eyes from my toe-caps all I could see was pit-head wheels and factory chimneys, but in Robert Frost's poem 'Out, Out —'

> . . . those that lifted eyes could count
> Five mountain ranges one behind the other
> Under the sunset far into Vermont.

'Out, Out —' is a fine poem, one of the first to draw me towards the craft of the poet. Despite his rather traditional scene-setting Frost's poem goes on to communicate the emotion of a horrifying moment.

One of the problems with emotional communication is that the response depends on who the story is told to. The story of the rugby match will be far better received by a friend than by the average grandmother or auntie.

It's the same with poetry. The poem is received with a different reaction by different people. That was the first lesson I began to learn when I started to write.

I wrote 'Ring Song' to try to tell something of what I believe the poet's role to be — the passing on of stories. I feel the process is never-ending. The poet will continue to pass on the story as long as there are ears to hear.

The story of Arthur Prance belongs to America in the 1930s. At that time dancers were superstars — much as pop singers are today. There was no television then but there were dance-halls, there was cinema.

Most of the stars are forgotten now, but men like Bill 'Bojangles' Robinson and Earl 'Snakehips' Tucker were legends in their own lifetime. Arthur Prance was a small-time dance instructor, not one of the big time operators. Perhaps the reason Prance stayed in the minor league was because he was fat. Prance weighed over 300 lbs. (Almost $21\frac{1}{2}$ stone in English!)

We all get used to the idea that fat people are happy, that dancers are happy. Here was someone who was a fat dancer, yet he took his own life by jumping from a skyscraper in New York City.

'The Television Poem' was written after I passed a TV showroom on a pedestrian precinct in Swindon. It was very late, there was nobody about, but in the showroom window four television sets were showing the same picture. On each screen the same person was blabbing on about something or other but I couldn't hear a word.

It made me realise that one of the blessings about poetry is that it remains a very personal means of communication in an age which is dominated by the mass media. If you write a poem it's not going to get across to millions, for an instant, and then be instantly forgotten.

It might seem selfish to suggest that the poet should write a poem for himself — pass on *his* story entirely to *his* satisfaction. But I do believe that's the best way to go about it. You're not alone in the world and if you write a poem to satisfy yourself it's going to satisfy others like you. *Most* people might not hear it, read it. But if it's *most* people you're after, meaning the majority, there's no point in trying poetry to get across. It won't!

'Neap Tide' is a private poem — it's almost a diary entry. Long after I left Leigh I settled, for a time, in Robin Hood's Bay, the Yorkshire-coast fishing village.

One day I was down on the shore when I noticed something very different about the way the tide went out. It took its time, didn't lap or slap, but just got thinner and thinner very very slowly — rather like the ageing process. Later I worked out why. This was the neap, the autumnal tide when, 'solar and lunar attractions are combined or at right angles'. That's the dictionary definition.

I trust this little four-liner with its a, a b, b rhyme scheme has managed to communicate an emotion rather better than the fact.

The Television Poem

(for Patrick Taggart)

It is midnight.
You are passing the window
of a television showroom —
the door is barred,
a wire grille is in the window.
The shop is closed.

This poem is being transmitted to you
from inside the television showroom.
This poem comes to you twice in colour,
twice in black and white.
This poem is 625 line.
This poem is 21 inches
across the diagonal.

You do not hear this poem —
for all you know
this poem could be forecasting ice.
This poem could be telling of the world's end,
this poem could, conceivably,
be singing.

You will see this poem
but will fail to recognise it.
You will not hear this poem
without straining to hear it.
This poem is a mouth opening and closing
and opening and closing
and opening. O.

This poem is subliminal —
dismiss it.
This poem is ephemeral
and eminently passable.
Pass this poem —
let the poem be.

This poem is not for you.
This is my poem,
it is private.
Do not halt in your tracks for this poem.
Go about your business.
See her home.
See yourself home.

You will go home, together or alone.
You will sleep, together or alone.
In the morning you will awaken
and will forget every word of this poem.
There is nothing to remember.
There is nothing to forget.

You will not hear this poem.
This happens to most poems.

Neap Tide

Today the rock does not concede
To sea. The sea does not recede
From rock which worries through the weave,
An elbow through a threadbare sleeve.

Elegy for Arthur Prance—

'The Man Who Taught the Stars to Dance'

The toes that tapped through morning air
were once stand-ins for Fred Astaire.
The heels cool in the gutter where
the dancer lies up-ended.

    The one time only Arthur Prance —
    'The Man Who Taught The Stars to Dance' —
    had reached his zenith with a jig
    which once came over very big
    on radio.

The feet that clicked from ten flights high
and danced flamenco down the sky
had once made Ginger Rogers cry
'His *entrechat* is splendid.'

    The one time only Arthur Prance —
    'The Man Who Taught The Stars To Dance' —
    possessed an act of wide appeal
    especially his eightsome reel
    danced alone.

    The one time only Arthur Prance —
    'The Man Who Taught The Stars To Dance' —
    performed his final pirouette
    and heard applause he didn't get.

Ring Song

Once upon a time there was a story
It was not a long story. . .
It was a short story. . .
A good story. . .

It had neither a beginning, a middle
Or an end. . .

First of all the story was told to a child —
The child smiled and said *'Tell me another'*

And the story was told to a man of influence —
The man of influence ignored it

The story was told to a critic —
The critic stuffed his shirt with it

The story was told to a theologian —
The theologian doubted

The story was told to a soldier —
The soldier tore off its wings
And wore them on his helmet

The story was told to a historian —
'These are not facts' said the historian

The story was told to a politician —
The politician also smiled but said nothing

The story was told to a government
Who debated it, amended it —
And, finally, refused to pass it

The story was told to a policeman —
The policeman took out his notebook

The story was told to a judge
'What is a story?' asked the judge

The story was told to the hangman
Who wove it in his rope like hair

The story was told to a man in chains
Who made good his escape in it

The story was told to a juggler
Who threw it in the air and caught it
and threw it in the air and caught it
and threw it in the air. . .

The story was told to an acrobat
Who suspended it below him

The story was told to a sculptor
Who hammered it into the shape of his mother

The story was told to a painter
Who signed it in the corner
And hung it on the wall

And the story was told to a man of the sea
Who opened the story and sailed out upon it

The story was told to a young girl
Whose mirror it became

The story was told to a bird —
The bird built a nest in its branches

And the story was told to a poet
And the poet passed on the story

And this was the story. . .

Once upon a time there was a story
It was not a long story. . .
It was a short story. . .
A good story. . .

It had neither a beginning, a middle
Or an end. . .

The Television Poem

The stanzas of this poem alternate between six and seven lines in length, with an *envoi* (a shorter signing-off stanza) of two lines. The subject treated here is the possibly common feeling among writers that what they are trying to say may not communicate as clearly as they would like, or reach as many people as they would wish. There are barriers between a poet and his potential audience, represented here by the metaphor of the television showroom seen from outside at night. This is a familiar image for many people; most of us will have passed a lighted window of this kind and seen any number of screens with pictures as reproductions of each other, varying only in size, tone, or colour. The incongruousness of *hearing* the street sounds of the real world, and *seeing* scenes which you *cannot* hear, can have a real fascination. On these occasions, how much do we feel the need to hear the commentary? Is this perhaps an instance of television actually allowing our imaginations to work freely? Does it normally do this? Do you think the metaphor works as applied to poems and poets?

There may be scope here for writing a poem arising out of looking into any lighted window (shops, offices, private homes, buses) as an outsider.

Ring Song

This is an example of one kind of pattern poem: there is a pre-determined idea and pattern for each stanza. The 'story' is told to a different person each time; and each person (according to Pete Morgan) has a different outlook on life which affects what he does with it, and forms the second part of each verse. It is a question of thinking of a kind of person, and then deciding what the individual reaction of that person would be.

The poem is mainly written in couplets (pairs of lines) and often employs wordplay — 'the critic stuffed his shirt with it' — or witty, caustic comments on the life of the person. It has been given the title 'Ring Song' (and has actually been printed in a circle on one occasion) because the end of the poem returns to the words of the beginning, in a never-ending circle. Perhaps you know the rhyme 'The Bear Went Over the Mountain', which is similar in that — in theory at least — it never ends?

Try writing a pattern poem of your own. You will need an idea: for example, a window through which different people look and see what they want to see; a camera with which different people choose to take particular photographs; or a dream which varies according to the dreamer. There are all sorts of possibilities; simply write what happens. Your poem may end differently from 'Ring Song', or it may return to its beginning.

Neap Tide

This four-line poem is written to a regular rhythmic and rhyming pattern. Each line is iambic in rhythm, with four heavy stresses:

Tŏdaý/thĕ róck/ doĕs nót/cŏncéde

— although lines 1 and 2 run on to the next lines, so that when you read the poem for its sense, the rhythm of the lines is less obvious. Lines 1 and 2 rhyme, and so do lines 3 and 4. The vowel sound that is most noticeable is 'e', as 'in concede', 'sea', 'recede', 'weave' and 'sleeve'. This is a soft, calming sound, such as might suggest the sound of the neap tide at this point.

There is a hint of a haiku here, but in an English form. This short poem captures a picture, echoes the sound, and leaves us with a haunting image of 'an elbow through a threadbare sleeve'. You may have tried writing haiku in the past; perhaps this form of the quatrain in iambic rhythm (with or without rhymes) might give you just that little extra scope to play around with a picture and an idea. It is said that the iambic rhythm is more suited to spoken English. See what you think.

Elegy for Arthur Prance

An elegy is a poem mourning the death of someone or something, and is nearly always a tribute to them. In this case the elegy commemorates one Arthur Prance, a dancing instructor who tragically committed suicide by jumping from a skyscraper. It is written in rhyme, but with lines not always of the same length, and a rhyme scheme that is not the same for each stanza. Play has been made with the fact that Prance was a dancer, and terms from dancing are used to describe events. This is a technique you might like to practise yourself — it has some similarities to the use of extended metaphor. If there is someone, or better still some *thing*, you are sorry to feel is no longer with us, you may like to think of writing an elegy. Older people often mourn the passing of things like trams, or steam engines, or pounds, shillings and pence, or family singsongs round the piano, or their own youth. Are you nostalgic about anything? In your own life, what has disappeared — or is about to disappear — which you regret, and may 'mourn' for?

George MacBeth

I began writing poems when I was six, and stopped when I was nine.
My mother kept early verses sewn together into a thin booklet, but
when I re-started writing poetry at the age of sixteen, encouraged by a
lively school English master with a taste — and a skill — for reading
aloud, the booklet had disappeared, and I can no longer remember
what my first efforts were about. I doubt if they were much good, but I
have a faint feeling that one described a hen. Certainly birds and
beasts (wild as well as domestic) have remained a major pre-
occupation, not only, I think, for their own sakes, but because the
extremity and crisis of their lives — often more threatened than
ours — offer dire warnings and vivid symbols. Indeed, animals play
a significant role in three of the poems here, trailing their splendour,
and their corpses.

'When I am Dead' is, I think, the earliest of my poems in this anthology. It arose from the experience of planning to make a will, and suddenly feeling (after receiving a bank statement and seeing a doctor) too poor and too healthy for the legacy-bequeathing to seem timely. The poem tries to capture the slightly unreal self-glamourising (a macabre and almost Monty-Python-ish condition) which may sometimes accompany a ritual action. The poem was written very early in the morning, too, and scarcely at all revised, which may account for its rough-hewn and grumpy tone.

'The Red Herring' is a fairly literal translation from the French of a nineteenth century poet, Charles Cros, who was admired by the Surrealists. When I first read the original, I thought: Goodness me, I must have written this. Its teasing, lightly-structured pointlessness exactly matches a frequent mood of mine, one of annoyance with people who expect a poem to send its meaning popping up like a jack-in-the-box at the slightest twitch of a spring. The real meaning of a poem is a subtle thing, and it can't always be separated out from the flow of the rhythm or the coherence of the images.

'Bats' is about bats, now a protected species. I was trying to match the radar-controlled zig-zag of these phenomenal creatures in the running-on, looping and jerking of the poem's line structure. But no human ingenuity could equal these virtuoso acrobats who are, after all, far from batty.

'Snowdrops' is the most solemn and romantic of the poems. My wife and I bought an old house in Norfolk in late autumn and were delighted when January came to find that we had acquired a free bonus — a garden full of flowers. It was like opening the drawers of an old chest bought at a sale and finding them full of fine white linen. The poem tries to capture the surprise and joy of someone experiencing the freshness of a new start in life.

When I am Dead

I desire that my body be
properly clothed. In such things
as I may like at the time.

And in the pockets may there be
placed such things as I use at the time
as, pen, camera, wallet, file.

And I desire to be laid on my side
face down: since I have bad dreams
if I lie on my back.

No one shall see my face when I die.

And beside me shall lie
my stone pig
with holes in his eyes.

And the coffin shall be as big as a crate.
No thin box
for the bones only.

Let there be room for a rat to come in.

And see that my cat, if I have one then,
shall have my liver.
He will like that.

And lay in food for
a week and a day:
chocolate, meat, beans, cheese.

And let all lie in
the wind and the rain
And on the eighth day burn.

And the ash
scatter as the wind decides.
And the stone and metal be dug in the ground.

This is my will.

The Red Herring

after Cros

There was once a high wall, a bare wall. And
against this wall, there was a ladder,
a long ladder. And on the ground,
under the ladder, there was a red
herring. A dry red herring.

And then a man came along. And in his hands
(they were dirty hands) this man had
a heavy hammer, a long nail
(it was also a sharp nail) and
a ball of string. A thick ball of string.

All right. So the man climbed up
the ladder (right up to the top)
and knocked in the sharp nail:
spluk! Just like that.
Right on top of the wall. The bare wall.

Then he dropped the hammer. It dropped
right down to the ground. And onto the nail
he tied a piece of string, a long
piece of string, and onto the string
he tied the red herring. The dry red herring.

And let it drop. And then he climbed
down the ladder (right down
to the bottom), picked up the hammer
and also the ladder (which was pretty heavy)
and went off. A long way off.

And since then, that red herring, the dry
red herring on the end of the string, which is
quite a long piece, has been
very very slowly swinging and
swinging to a stop. A full stop.

I expect you wonder why I made
up this story, such a simple story. Well,
I did it just to annoy people.
Serious people. And perhaps also
to amuse children. Small children.

Bats

have no accidents. They loop
their incredible horse-shoe
loops, dead-stop

on air-brakes,
road-safe on
squeaks: racketeering

their SOS noise in a
jai-alai
bat-jam

of collapsed umbrellas, a
Chancery Lane
of avoided

collisions, all in a
cave without lights: then
hung

happy, a snore
of strap-hangers
undergrounding

without an *Evening
Standard* between them
to the common Waterloo

that awaits bats, like
all beasts, then
off now, zoom!

Man, you can't even
hear them; bats,
are they?

Snowdrops

The first day of this month I saw
Their active spearheads. Dry and raw

They rose from grass, beside my pond,
In a white stockade. And now, beyond

Far evergreens, more gather, and
Advance on dead ground. Dour they stand,

As if numb earth depended on
Their stolid hold. And what has gone,

Or will go, when they give, means time.
Time to be emptying ponds of slime,

Time to be slow, time to work hard.
I see them thicken, yard by yard.

These are the first of our strong flowers.
Before the spring, or April showers,

They teem with loyalty, and fight
For a place in the sun. Static in flight

Their icy lances pierce with green
Last year's downed leaves. I touch one. Clean

And moist upon my reaching palm,
I feel its energy, its calm.

When I am Dead

The idea of writing a will is very ancient. People who feel they must 'stage-manage' this part of their lives (or deaths) enjoy the opportunities it provides. For the poet, however, there are more creative possibilities. George MacBeth has written here about what should be done with his own body. He is not especially interested in possessions left to others — except, of course, for bequeathing his liver to his cat. As he indicates in his introduction, he has tried to reflect some of the self-aggrandisement that making a will seems to carry with it, a certain self-indulgence. You might have ideas along similar lines for a poem of your own. Or you might like to write a poetic will leaving various things to people whom you know, or who are in the public eye. The things you leave would preferably not be money and property, but unusual possessions, and concepts like courage, humility, your memories, or your laughter and sorrow.

The Red Herring

This poem is written in a chatty style, with phrases repeated, and short sentences. Sentences start anywhere in the lines, but the line-endings are very effective. Notice how many of the lines end in a way that 'tumbles' you on to the next line; for example:

> And then he climbed down
> the ladder (right down to the bottom) . . .

The story told is reminiscent of surrealist paintings or films, which jolt us out of complacency and disturb the expected sequence of events. Incongruous objects are placed in ordinary landscapes, or people suddenly do something wholly strange, or events take a highly unusual turn. The title of this poem is a colloquial expression which means 'something irrelevant'. This helps to suggest that what the man does is irrelevant also — or does it? You might imitate this style in writing your own surreal poem. One way to approach this might be to take a common expression as your title: 'A Cock-and-Bull Story', 'A Blessing in Disguise', 'One Eye on the Clock', 'The White Lie', or 'Stick-in-the-Mud'. If you are very clever you will weave a story or picture around the expression which could also illustrate its meaning.

Bats

You might like to compare this poem with the one about bats by John Mole on page 109. As George MacBeth suggests in his introduction, he tried to use a form that would reflect the movements of these creatures. The stanzas are short, and regular in length, perhaps representing the almost pattern-like regularity of the bats' flight, back and forth, over your head in the dusk. Notice how he has used images of London in his description:

> a snore
> of strap-hangers
> undergrounding
>
> without an *Evening*
> *Standard* between them
> to the common Waterloo
>
> that awaits bats

They are like commuters making for Waterloo Station on their way home. The other meaning of 'meeting one's Waterloo' is of course, to suffer a great defeat, or even meet one's end.

Snowdrops

This is written in rhyming couplets (pairs of lines that rhyme) and in a predominantly iambic tetrameter rhythm (tetrameter means four heavy stresses, or beats) for each line. To stop the iambic rhythm becoming monotonous it is necessary to vary the way each line must be read. This can be achieved by finishing and starting sentences in the middle of lines, or letting the sense run over from one line to another. 'Snowdrops' is a very good example of this, but have you noticed how some lines are not completely iambic either? For example:

> For a place in the sun. Static in flight

Why not try writing a poem in this form? It will be good practice in using rhyme and rhythm — but do not use just *any* word to rhyme or you will spoil the effect. What you have to say is all-important, so if you cannot find a suitable rhyme, try rephrasing the whole idea, so that another word occurs at the end of the line. It is rather like a jigsaw puzzle. You may have to search for quite a while for the correct piece; but only that one will fit, and it is no use trying to force another one into the gap.

John Birtwhistle

My father wrote books and sermons, my mother had read English at university, and of course our house was full of books. But you could say the same for my brother and sisters, who don't claim to be poets. The difference with me, for reasons so deep I hardly understand them myself, was that I always had an oddly personal feeling for all these words that surrounded us. I was curious about them, rather worried about them, impressed by them. I enjoyed playing and experimenting with them on paper as though they were not just marks but living shapes.

In my teens, the poetry of the past — especially Blake and Shelley — became important to me because it seemed to reflect my own attitudes on matters like politics, religion, nature and the authorities of daily life. I escaped from my boarding school carrying a volume of Shelley, and found myself in a day school where three or four pupils were writing music and poetry as though it were a normal and reasonable thing to do. What was more, the English master took a patient interest in what we wrote, commented practically on our verses, pointed us to all sorts of reading and, as a published poet himself, gave one something to aim for. By the time I left school I had three publishable poems.

About the poems in this book: My 'Hitch-hiker's Curse' comes out of many hours spent thumbing lifts when it used to be rather safer to do so than it is now. You used to be bored and resentful most of the time, then suddenly excited when a car or lorry looked like stopping. Sometimes you were really left in the lurch. At such times you hated the privilege of the car-owners — although, of course, you'd be very willing to accept it yourself if only they'd stop for you. Curses go back to the origins of poetry, because they are a magical use of words: simply pronouncing them seems to have power. Something of this ancient magic also attaches to riddles. There is a kind of Anglo-Saxon verse riddle, in which the object — the answer to the riddle — is given a teasing voice of its own. These poems attract me because the very act of giving a voice to an onion, or hen, or clothespeg, is an odd and intriguing thing to do. It gives intelligence to things we had taken for granted and hardly noticed.

The Hitch-hiker's Curse on Being Passed by

(Excerpts)

The Curse of Your Wheels to you!
May your inlet manifold get choked
While your head gaskets are leaking
And may your camshaft lobes wear out.
Although your cylinders each crack,
A man will be found to replace them,
Wrecking as he does so your valve stem seals
And knocking your tappet clearances awry.
No fruit of your driving: your plugs never dry,
Your tanks never wet — nor those of your daughters.
Trail a long lorry loaded with logs. . .

Speeding to get you nowhere, slowing down
To bring you neither calm nor safety.
Stones to puncture, sheep to stand stubborn
In your path. Dull bulls to dent your doors
As ever forking lanes confound your way.
May your turnings left end all at sea
Unless into quicksand; your rights into mines
Or else onto firing range. May you backfire
And blow the crook from the fist of St Pancras
To bring down all His curses on your neck.
Seven terriers to snarl at your inner tubes.
Rest at last in a black bog, whereupon
A slide of boulders to bury your wheels and you. . .

Crawl, you may as well, up your own silencer,
For be assured: you will come by no agony
But that you will survive to suffer it,
Your fate a mystery to your own people.

Riddle

I am something
that has been changed

Once I was green and springy
Then I was brown and tough
Next I was red and brittle
At last I am soft and grey

I am so light
one snowflake does not rest
so gently upon another

so gentle that one
downy feather is not so light
against another
on a pigeon's breast

I have been changed indeed
and now I am finished

Once green and lively
I have been made use of
and now they treat me like dirt

a light grey slight soft and falling thing
yet if you weighed me in the balance
you would find me of more weight
than that from which I was made

Who am I then?
Tell me quick
before I am brushed away

(ʍood ɥs∀)

The Hitch-hiker's Curse on Being Passed by

This poem, which revels in the language of cars and engines, is almost an orgy of a curse. It resembles some ancient curses and spells (except that it does not rhyme), and bears little relation to the obscene and repetitive language often used today when somebody swears and curses. How much more inventive and ultimately satisfying it would be to curse in the manner of this hitch-hiker. Whether it would be more, or less, offensive to the victim is hard to say. But at least it might give him pause for thought while your imagination ran riot.

Can you think of a frustrating situation in which you needed to vent your feelings somehow? Perhaps someone took something of yours, or ate the last chocolate cake? Or you were prevented by accident from taking part in something? There are plenty of occasions, ranging from the mildest to the most serious, when we are irritated or downright angry, and need an outlet. Can you write a witty and imaginative curse? Try to use the language of the situation, as John Birtwhistle has with the language of cars and driving.

Riddle

Riddles have been around a long time. The Anglo-Saxons particularly loved them — there are many examples which are beautiful and intriguing to read. The poem-riddle, however, sets out to describe something in interesting and colourful language, in a way that lays clues to the identity of the object described. In writing such a poem you must be careful not to make guessing too easy (but also not too difficult!). There must be enough clues, but your readers want the satisfaction of being Sherlock Holmes. *How* you describe your subject, what metaphors and similes you employ, will decide the success of your riddle in the end. Many older ones rhyme, and were full of superstition, supposed impossibilities, hints of magic. Here is one of the most famous:

> In marble walls as white as milk,
> Lined with a skin as soft as silk,
> Within a fountain crystal clear,
> A golden apple doth appear.
> No doors there are to this stronghold —
> Yet thieves break in and steal the gold.

> *Traditional*
>
> (ᙠᨂᨂ)

Ted Hughes

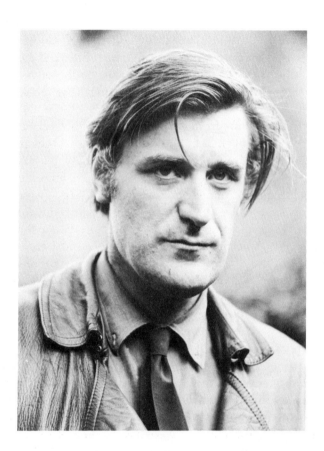

As I remember it, I began to take an interest in writing when I went to grammar school. I found I could amuse my classmates with it, and even sometimes my teacher, as well as myself. So I was eleven. In those early days I wrote about fantastic happenings in the Canadian Forests, the Wild West, in tropical jungles, and in Africa — places well away from the South Yorkshire town we lived in and the gloom of the war which hung over us.

At that time, and for some years after, I thought about little but shooting, trapping and fishing, and birds, animals and fish. I spent most of my spare time trying to make contact with the wild life — of which there was quite a lot — in the fields and woods on the other side of the river Don, to the south of the town. Naturally, I was reading all I could find about this sort of thing, but in those days the books were not so plentiful — the big, beautiful volumes of natural history, which are now so common, did not exist. So a little had to go a long way. I read *Tarka the Otter* over and over constantly for two years. I remember trying to imitate in my writing that book's magic atmosphere.

Rhymes intrigued me from early on. I remember very clearly the moment I realised that rhymes made a difference — they made your writing feel special. But my versifying didn't really get going until I encountered Kipling's *Complete Poems*, when I was about fourteen. I don't know what drew me to Kipling. Probably *The Jungle Book*, his story of Mowgli, the boy among the animals, which our teacher had read to us in class. I remember the look of the book, the *Complete Poems*, there on the shelf, in the town library, and I took it down. Kipling's tramping drumbeat rhythms evidently gave me a shock. From that point, I began to write my tales in verse — in Kipling's lockstep rhythms and resounding, deadlock rhymes:

'And the curling lips of the five gouged rips in the bark of the pine
were the mark of the bear'

was one of my lines.

For some time, my new interest in 'poetry' was limited almost completely to things written in this way. The only other book, at that time, which gave me similar satisfaction was the Bible. I read it through like a novel, looking for great moments, trying to learn by heart the ones I liked best. My English teachers were having their effect, and by the time I entered the Sixth Form, at fifteen, my school life — what I remember of it — revolved round our three set books: Shakespeare's *King Lear*, Shelley's *Adonais*, and Thomas Hardy's *The Woodlanders*. Through these, I became aware of what lay beyond metre, rhythm and rhyme.

One influence, that I am sure helped me to take the decisive step, might seem a strange one. Somewhere around the age of thirteen I had discovered the existence of folktales. Collecting tales, legends and myths became my craze. That kind of literature was also scarce in those days, but the rarity made me keener. It so happened, that the tales, legends, etc., that stirred me most were the Irish. I was spell-bound by the strange, intense world they created. And at the height of this obsession I found a writer with the same obsession — the poet W.B. Yeats. I swallowed whole his passion for Irish folktales, legends and myths. And in return, his poetry digested me. Everybody who gets there finds his own way into the world of poetic imagination. This odd roundabout route was mine.

In the three poems here, the folktale background is very easy to see. In 'The Seven Sorrows', for instance, the very title is borrowed from the world of folk legends. And each of the seven verses is like a little scene from a folktale — as it might be a scene from a fable in a stained glass window. In the first verse, the tale might be called 'How The Dead Tried to Remain With The Living'. In the second, the story might be called 'The Forest That Tried To Be A Bird'. The third might be called, 'The Lost Wager'. It wouldn't be difficult to invent the stories that would fit these titles — stories which would include the scenes in the verses. So each verse is a fragment of its own story, but is at the same time both, a metaphor for some sad aspect of autumn and a real thing typical of autumn.

'The Golden Boy' is slightly different. It reminds the reader that it is a remaking of the popular folksong 'John Barleycorn'. But the folklore behind it goes back to the source of that song. In ancient times, people thought of the corn as a god who gave them life. If the corn failed to grow, if for some reason it withered that year and failed to produce its miracle of food, the people would starve to death. Just as is happening at present in various parts of the world. The corn was so important, in fact, that it would not be saying too much to say that the people worshipped it. Before this god could give them life, they had to persuade him to grow, with care and kindness and worship. But then they had to kill him. That is, they had to cut him down, and grind the grain. And because their lives depended on it, this became a religious ritual: worshipping the god as he grew to his full strength, then killing and eating him. 'John Barleycorn' is a comic song, because it tells how this great life-giving god was killed, in this case, not to provide food for people who would die without it, but to make strong drink — the Barley Ale which makes the drinkers drunk. And the drunkards sing this song. But I retell the story as it was in the beginning, when the corn god was killed for food that was known to be vital. The meaning of this becomes quite clear to people anywhere, when they are faced with famine. And famine, as we know, belongs to the present and the future, just as much as to the most ancient past.

In the poem 'Leaves' I have adapted a nursery rhyme which everybody will recognise. In my poem, the leaves are the spirit of the living year. Again, each verse is part of a little fable, and each verse brings its fable to the story of the funeral of the leaves. At the same time, of course, each verse has to fit the real facts of autumn. The river's great floods, which cleanse the banks and the bed, come in autumn, and are thick with dead leaves, and bury many of these leaves under silt in deep backwaters. The tractor ploughs the stubble after harvest, in autumn. The robin begins, in autumn, to sing a particularly haunting and thrilling song. So the poem is a rosary of autumnal happenings, but in the form of a folktale.

The Seven Sorrows

The first sorrow of autumn
Is the slow goodbye
Of the garden who stands so long in the evening —
A brown poppy head,
The stalk of a lily,
And still cannot go.

The second sorrow
Is the empty feet
Of the pheasant who hangs from a hook with his brothers.
The woodland of gold
Is folded in feathers
With its head in a bag.

And the third sorrow
Is the slow goodbye
Of the sun who has gathered the birds and who gathers
The minutes of evening,
The golden and holy
Ground of the picture.

The fourth sorrow
Is the pond gone black
Ruined and sunken the city of water —
The beetle's palace,
The catacombs
Of the dragonfly.

And the fifth sorrow
Is the slow goodbye
Of the woodland that quietly breaks up its camp.
One day it's gone.
It has left only litter —
Firewood, tentpoles.

And the sixth sorrow
Is the fox's sorrow
The joy of the huntsman, the joy of the hounds,
The hooves that pound
Till earth closes her ear
To the fox's prayer.

And the seventh sorrow
Is the slow goodbye
Of the face with its wrinkles that looks through the window
As the year packs up
Like a tatty fairground
That came for the children.

The Golden Boy

In March he was buried
    And nobody cried
Buried in the dirt
    Nobody protested
Where grubs and insects
    That nobody knows
With outer-space faces
    That nobody loves
Can make him their feast
    As if nobody cared.

But the Lord's mother
    Full of her love
Found him underground
    And wrapped him with love
As if he were her baby
    Her own born love
She nursed him with miracles
    And starry love
And he began to live
    And to thrive on her love

He grew night and day
    And his murderers were glad
He grew like a fire
    And his murderers were happy
He grew lithe and tall
    And his murderers were joyful
He toiled in the fields
    And his murderers cared for him
He grew a gold beard
    And his murderers laughed.

With terrible steel
    They slew him in the furrow
With terrible steel
    They beat his bones from him
With terrible steel
    They ground him to powder
They baked him in ovens
    They sliced him on tables
They ate him they ate him
    They ate him they ate him
Thanking the Lord
Thanking the Wheat
Thanking the Bread
For bringing them Life
Today and Tomorrow
Out of the dirt.

Leaves

Who's killed the leaves?
Me, says the apple, I've killed them all.
Fat as a bomb or a cannonball
I've killed the leaves.

Who sees them drop?
Me, says the pear, they will leave me all bare
So all the people can point and stare.
I see them drop.

Who'll catch their blood?
Me, me, me, says the marrow, the marrow.
I'll get so rotund that they'll need a wheelbarrow.
I'll catch their blood.

Who'll make their shroud?
Me, says the swallow, there's just time enough
Before I must pack all my spools and be off.
I'll make their shroud.

Who'll dig their grave?
Me, says the river, with the power of the clouds
A brown deep grave I'll dig under my floods.
I'll dig their grave.

Who'll be their parson?
Me, says the Crow, for it is well-known
I study the bible right down to the bone.
I'll be their parson.

Who'll be chief mourner?
Me, says the wind, I will cry through the glass
The people will pale and go cold when I pass.
I'll be chief mourner.

Who'll carry the coffin?
Me, says the sunset, the whole world will weep
To see me lower it into the deep.
I'll carry the coffin.

Who'll sing a psalm?
Me, says the tractor, with my gear grinding glottle
I'll plough up the stubble and sing through my throttle.
I'll sing the psalm.

Who'll toll the bell?
Me, says the robin, my song in October
Will tell the still gardens the leaves are over.
I'll toll the bell.

The Seven Sorrows

In his introduction, Ted Hughes suggests that each verse is a scene from a folk tale, and he gives possible titles for the stories told by the first three. You might like to try inventing ingenious or mysterious titles for the rest of the verses.

This is an example of a pattern poem (see also the other poems in this section, and Pete Morgan's section, pages 66–75). The first line of each stanza has the same form, and the title gives the number of stanzas in the whole poem. The other ingredient in this pattern is the theme of autumn. Each stanza describes a different facet of autumn and what it represents — the dying away of the natural year. In writing such a poem, a pattern of this kind can be very helpful in providing a frame-work so that you can concentrate on each verse individually. Then the overall theme virtually looks after itself.

You can try writing your own poem on the idea of change, be it growth, decay, or simply things altering as time passes. For example, you could write the Seven Sorrows of Man, or Woman, the Seven Joys of Spring, the Seven Ages of Man (after the famous passage in Shakespeare), the Twelve Ages of a Year, the Phases of the Moon (during a month of waxing and waning), or any other theme of your own. Try to incorporate any legends or superstitions you know, but keep the images concrete rather than abstract. Describe the pictures and metaphors in precise and exciting language (notice Ted Hughes's lines in the seventh verse: 'As the year packs up/Like a tatty fairground/That came for the children').

The Golden Boy

As explained in Ted Hughes's introduction, the original pattern or rhyme is an old folk song, 'John Barleycorn', which you may have come across. But Ted Hughes has written his poem out of an even older tradition — that of the bread of life. Although we do not obviously worship such necessities any more in the West (though in parts of the world people still do) we nevertheless retain the remnants of such beliefs. We have certain superstitious customs, such as the making of corn dollies. We also have rather more modern 'gods', like money, sun-worship (think of all the sunbathers), and more dreadful talismans or charms like nuclear weapons. Different members of a society will 'worship' different things. For example, farmers may pray for sun to ripen the harvest, or at haymaking time; sailors used to pray for a breeze for the sails, and stars for steering; and fishermen might pray that the fish will rise to their bait. If we do not obtain these things we say we are unlucky, which implies that we feel 'the gods are against us'. In much earlier times people worshipped the life-giving gods and made sacrifices to them — the all-important sun, the rain, the seasons of the year, food plants, apple trees, etc. You may be able to find out customs and traditions associated with these which are still practised (for example, the Druids' ceremony on midsummer morning at Stonehenge and the pouring of a libation in cider apple orchards to ensure a good crop).

Leaves

Here is another kind of pattern based on the old rhyme, 'Who killed Cock Robin?' 'I', said the sparrow, 'With my bow and arrow.' It is quite acceptable to take a rhyme you know, and use its pattern to write your own poem. You are not writing a parody — a satirical re-working of the original — but creating a completely new and serious poem out of the form of another.

Obviously an old, traditional rhyme which contains repetition, or a refrain (or chorus) provides a good pattern for you to use. Rhymes like 'The House that Jack Built', 'This Little Pig Went to Market', 'Here We Go Round the Mulberry Bush', and many other nursery rhymes or old folk songs, can become quite new and unusual when their patterns are used for a different purpose. If you wish, you can employ the same rhythms and rhyme scheme. All you need to concentrate on is what you have to say, and how you can fit it into the framework provided for you. Find a theme for the whole poem and feel free to experiment with your pattern; even to alter or extend it. For example, if you were writing about spring using the 'Little Pig' rhyme, you might begin with, 'This little seed fell on soft ground'. You might then follow this with a few lines to describe what happens next. The next verse might begin with, 'This little seed fell on stone'. The third verse might be, 'This little seed blew away on the wind', and the fourth, 'This little seed hasn't grown'. And so on, each line beginning a verse which expands the description. If wanted, the first lines could be gathered together to make a final verse-cum-refrain.

John Mole

I had a West Country childhood. Home, until I went away to university, was Somerset, and holiday — the annual, two-week seaside ritual — was Devon. My father was a chartered accountant and did the books for an hotel in Torquay. He got on very well with the manager. They became close friends, so down we all went every August. Each year I saw the sea and paddled about in it but wasn't to cross the horizon for a long while to come. Abroad for us was Scotland (once) and Wales (twice). *Parochial* might be a word to describe this small compass, but not *limited*. I'm sure there is some connection between the fact that, while growing up, I never went geographically far afield, and my habit now of brooding very intently on what is close at hand. Or, to put it another way, if you stay in the same room long enough you become familiar with the furniture. It is something of an event if you re-position a mirror or put a chair in a different place.

When I look back on the 'room' of my childhood I certainly don't recall a bland sameness. It is not, as one poet called his early years, a 'forgotten boredom'. Rather, I seem to be drawn back to luminous particulars — holding them again, so to speak, in the palm of my imagination, turning them over and over, feeling their shape, celebrating their precious ordinariness until — when the time is right — the words come for a poem. The poem may not be *about* them but, somehow, they have put me in touch with the poem. My words seem to come alive when the ghost of who I was reminds me, suddenly, of who I am. These are difficult things to write about. It's easier to comment on individual poems. Easy, for example, to tell you that 'Reflections' is a sequence of six *cinquains*. The *cinquain* is a verse form invented by the American poet Adelaide Crapsey. It consists of five lines of two, four, six, eight, and two syllables, and is similar in its method of compressing thought or perception to the Japanese *haiku* with which you may be more familiar. I mentioned my habit of intent brooding. What can be more intent than reflection upon one's own reflection! You might try doing this — although you will need to keep a sense of humour and perspective. My favourite poem about looking at oneself in the mirror is 'The Face in the Mirror' by Robert Graves.

'Bats' is what the French call a *donnée*, and it was a French poet who gave it to me. I had been translating a group of *Chantefables* by Robert Desnos — humorous, wise little poems about animals — and when I finished I found I couldn't stop. The word-play in 'Bats' — 'vicarious areas', 'precarious', etc . — is very much by courtesy of Desnos, as is the mixture of jokiness and melancholy. Very Gallic, I think. There's nothing quite like it in English. The nearest thing — I suppose — would be the work of Edward Lear, another of my favourite poets.

My original title for 'First Snow' was 'Snow in January' because that was when it fell, and because I wrote it for a junior school class I was visiting in the same month. Titles are very important, and I changed this one in order to emphasise that the speaker is a child experiencing snow for the first time. Quite often I find this happening. I begin with an impulse, work it out through the poem, and end up playing around with the title. Poems are like cats. The naming of them is a difficult matter.

'Song of the Diplomat', though, began with a picture. My wife is an artist, and recently she produced a series of etchings based on European toys. Some of them were really quite sinister, and one of

them I found particularly so. It was a German toy called 'The Tra-
veller' — a doll-like man in a heavy overcoat pushing along a sort of
trunk-on-wheels. He looked to me like the kind of anonymous sur-
vivor who always finds himself on the right side. Place him in a hot
political situation and he'll manage to reckon the odds in his favour.
The repetitive, circular patterning of the poem reinforces, I hope, the
point I'm making. You can't tell whether this diplomatic opportunist
is coming or going. All you can tell is that he keeps on the move. Is he
a man of the people or a Party Member? Can one ever be both at the
same time? Perhaps this poem is not as playful as it may at first
appear.

Reflections

Mirror
On the wall, is
Yours the face ill-met each
Morning? Why is it less and less
Like mine?

Keep me
(You are welcome!)
But see that I behave.
People in glass houses shouldn't
Throw stones.

Those bags
Beneath the eyes
Are packed with weariness.
Too much overnight travelling
Caused that.

Now, though,
Is not the time
For such reflections.
Mirror, your kind was never meant
To think.

Neither
Mortal spy-glass
Nor prophetic crystal —
No, you cannot tell me anything
At all.

Easy
To walk away
From mirrors, harder though
To quite forget that what's still me
Was you.

First Snow

Whose is this long, unexpected elbow
Resting its white sleeve on the wall?
Is anyone out there when I call
To hear my voice? I've lost my echo.

Whose are these feathery tears that keep coming?
Somebody weeps without a sound
And leaves his grief heaped up on the ground.
It's so quiet my ears are drumming.

Whose is that handkerchief on the gatepost
Large enough for a giant sneeze?
Bless you whisper the shivering trees
While I just stand here like a ghost.

Who am I? And where have I woken?
It wasn't the same when I went to bed.
I still feel me inside my head
Though now a different language is spoken.

Suddenly all the meanings have gone.
Is someone trying to tell me something?
A bird shakes silver dust from its wing
And the sky goes on and on and on.

Song of the Diplomat

When the Party's losses are the People's gains
You'll find me near the border changing trains.

You'll find me near the border changing trains
When the blood runs free and the free blood stains.

When the blood runs free and the free blood stains
The People's losses are the Party's gains.

When the People's losses are the Party's gains
You'll find me near the border changing trains.

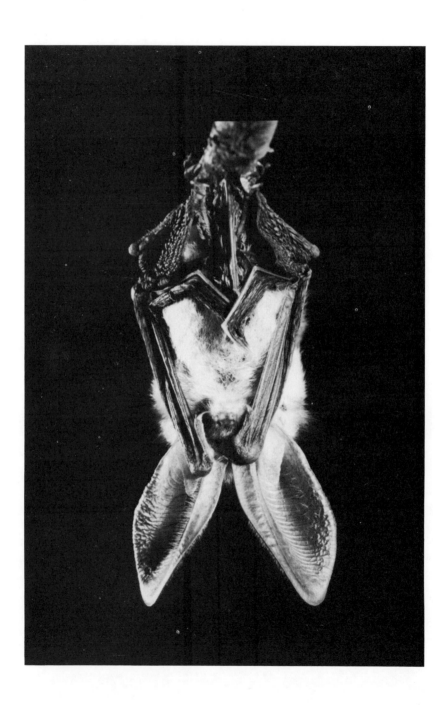

Bats

Bats like various
musty old areas:

belfries, of course,
where they rehearse

a crotchety score,
dangling galore

from cross-bar staves,
troubling graves

with the dark bells' boom
of their leather tune;

or a spooky loft
where dust lies soft

on forgotten things,
and someone sings

in her room below
that song bats know

whose notes contain
the squeak of pain; . . .

Oh, bats like various
vicarious areas,

preferably precarious.

Reflections

John Mole explains that each stanza of this poem is a cinquain, a form invented by an American poet called Adelaide Crapsey. A cinquain contains five lines, each with a set number of syllables: 2, 4, 6, 8 and 2. The rhythm should be iambic throughout (see page 118 for an explanation of iambic rhythm) but poets often vary this, so do not worry if you cannot sustain it in your own efforts. Because a cinquain is short, it is particularly useful for making you choose words carefully; you cannot afford to waste the few syllables at your disposal. One five-line cinquain can stand on its own as a poem, or you can write a longer piece where each separate stanza is a cinquain, as John Mole has done here. Notice how he has played with the meanings of words and phrases to suggest more than one meaning. 'Ill-met each morning' has echoes of 'Ill-met by moonlight, proud Titania', in Shakespeare's *A Midsummer Night's Dream*. 'People in glass houses' arises from the fact that mirrors are made of glass. 'Reflections' are thoughts as well as images in glass.

First Snow

This poem is written in four-line stanzas where the first and fourth lines rhyme, and the second and third lines rhyme (a, b, b, a; c, d, d, c; e, f, f, e; etc.) Notice the images John Mole uses to describe the snow and its effects: 'white sleeve', 'feathery tears', 'handkerchief'. Notice, too, how he goes on to use that image and extend the picture, so that the 'feathery tears', for example, lead into 'somebody weeps without a sound/ And leaves his grief heaped on the ground'. Try writing a poem to describe other possible first experiences of a child — perhaps a thunderstorm, a visit to the sea, or a train ride. The language you use will not be that of a child, but the images you choose will probably be of simple everyday things that a child would know.

Bats

'Bats' is written in rhyming couplets — that is to say, pairs of lines that rhyme — with the exception of the last single line which rhymes with the preceding pair. From its punctuation you will notice that the whole poem makes up just one sentence, the only full stop falling at the end. The first couplet states the fact upon which the rest of the poem elaborates. The main metaphors used are all musical ones, and this gives the poem its descriptive theme. 'Bats' shows a playful enjoyment of language and rhyme, particularly evident in the last three lines. 'Vicarious' also manages to suggest 'vicars', whose church belfries the bats might frequent. Can you write a poem on similar lines? You will need to choose a subject — an animal possibly? — and make a statement about it in the first couplet. The rest of the poem will go on to explore the possibilities thrown up by that statement.

Song of the Diplomat

This is a cleverly constructed poem which plays with the possibilities of language by using phrases that can be turned round and still make sense. There are basically only three lines used here, but by swapping the positions of the words new ideas are discovered. There is also a repetition of whole lines. Each rhyming couplet begins with the second line of the previous couplet. Only three different words are used in the rhyme pattern: *trains, gains* and *stains*. You might like to experiment with finding phrases or sentences where, by changing the word order, you create a new meaning; for example, 'the hope of ages lives in the age of hope', or 'the love of mankind can show the kind of man to love', or 'at the heart of darkness is the darkness of the heart.' You may begin to find you have an idea to expand into a poem by using this technique.

John Fuller

I began writing poems in the prep-room of my boarding school when I was sixteen. It didn't seem strange to do so. All kinds of things went on there: chess, attempts to get round the room without touching the floor, hiding oriental food in lockers, making home-made fireworks, the usual sort of thing. I was very interested in both films and surrealism at that time, and poetry had to compete. But almost immediately there came a chance to enter for a school poetry prize, for which I wrote, with a dizzy sense of discovery, a number of sonnets about death, highly moralizing and melodramatic. The less awful bits showed that I had been reading poets like de la Mare, Auden and Graves, and there is the spectre of Eliot peering over my shoulder in my first published poem, in *The Listener* later that year. It was to be eight years before I published a collection of poems. What did I learn from all this? That the thrill of writing is some guarantee of its personal value — but you have to work very hard to get written the poems that it is in you to write.

Although I love to write poems with stories to them, or poems about ideas, I find on occasion that poems arrive simply as a technical challenge. What would a poem of one line be like? The one-line form of 'Bilberries' is of my own invention. It has to be an iambic pentameter with two rhymes: the first pair come at the beginning and end of the line, and the second pair on either side of a strong caesura (or pause for breath) in the middle of the line. It's a bit like a couplet that's swallowed itself. The sardine poem was part of a series on how to open various kinds of tins. Poems about ordinary daily tasks *can* be interesting, though not necessarily more interesting than poems about important things. The sonnet 'In a Railway Compartment' turns the puzzles of Lewis Carroll into terrifying nightmares — though I'm sure he was too much of a gentleman ever to threaten little girls like this in reality. Perhaps the poem is suggesting that she imagines it all. And perhaps our imaginations provide ways in which we can adjust to strange desires and changes in our lives.

How to Open Sardines

You don't have to grope in a
Drawer for an opener:
Sardines have a key and a lock.
There's a horrible slit
That you fit on a lip,
And you turn like you're winding a clock.

It's blunt and it's bendable,
Thin and expendable,
Useless except for sardines.
You can easily lose it,
And just try to use it.
On cylinder-shaped tins of beans.

It functions for feasting
Just once (like a bee-sting)
And doesn't grow rust in a drawer.
It curls up with the tin
Till it's stuck fast within,
And can't ever be used any more.

Bilberries

Late in the season: reason then not to wait.

Frown as you climb: time to smile going down.

See the spring: ling lifts and is a bee.

Drop to your knees: pleased to be where you stop.

Blue under green: seen, and seen first, by you.

Linger on the scree: greed's purple finger.

In a Railway Compartment

Oxford to London, 1884:
Against the crimson arm-rest leaned a girl
Of ten, holding a muff, twisting a curl,
Drumming her heels in boredom on the floor
Until a white-haired gentleman who saw
She hated travelling produced a case
Of puzzles: 'Seven Germans run a race. . .
Unwind this maze, escape the lion's paw. . .
The princess must be lowered by her hair. . .'
The train entered a tunnel, shrieking, all
The lights went out and when he took her hand
She was the princess in the tower and
A lion faced her on the moonlit wall
Who roared and reached and caught and held her there.

How to Open Sardines

Written in three six-line stanzas, this poem is a very good example of
how to write about ordinary, mundane matters of living — and no
subject *is* too insignificant for a poem. The rhyme scheme is a, a, b, c,
c, b. As it is used here it presents some instances of how to produce a
rhyme using more than one word, a device which can be valuable in
any kind of poetry but is most often employed in humorous verse
(here, 'grope in a' rhymes with 'opener').

Why not enjoy yourself, as John Fuller clearly has in this poem, by
writing about something so ordinary that normally you do not even
notice it? Instead of the larger preoccupations of life, take a close look
at some small actions in familiar, everyday living. You might
consider one of the following: brushing your teeth, scratching your
back, setting an alarm clock, or sharpening a pencil.

Bilberries

As John Fuller explains in his introduction, the form of this poem is
his own invention. You can always invent your own form. However
many you know (for example, haiku, sonnets, acrostics, the rhyming
couplet) there is always scope for devising a new one. You can decide
the ingredients for yourself: how many lines, perhaps; what kind of
rhythm; where the rhymes are placed; or how many syllables to each
line. Or you may like to write a poem in this form of John Fuller's.

If you do, remember you need two pairs of rhymes for each line:
'*Late* in the *season: reason* then not to *wait*'. One pair of rhymes occurs
at the beginning and end of the line (*late* and *wait*), the other pair in the
middle (*season* and *reason*). If you want to copy this form exactly, you
will need to understand iambic rhythm. This is the rhythm of
'limping', that is, a light stress followed by a heavy one. Limp round
the room, feel the rhythm. Say the following and hear the rhythm:

> The boy stood on the burning deck

> 'Twas brillig and the slithy toves

> I want to be a wallaby,
> A wallaby like Willoughby

In John Fuller's poem you will notice that this iambic rhythm breaks
in the middle of each line between the rhyming pair of words — he
puts a colon there to indicate the change.

In a Railway Compartment

This poem is predominantly in the iambic rhythm, in pentameters. A pentameter is a line of five feet (an iambic foot is one light stress and one heavy):

$$\acute{\text{A}}\text{gainst/the cr}\acute{\text{i}}\text{m/s}\breve{\text{o}}\text{n a}\acute{\text{r}}\text{m/r}\breve{\text{e}}\text{st le}\acute{\text{a}}\text{ned/}\breve{\text{a}}\text{ g}\acute{\text{i}}\text{rl}$$
$$\quad\;1\qquad\;\;2\qquad\;\;3\qquad\quad4\qquad\;\;5$$

If you say this line out loud you will hear how the voice naturally stresses the syllables marked 1–5. So if you are writing in the iambic rhythm you need to choose words which when put together make you read in the right rhythm. This is not as difficult as it might sound. Try speaking to each other in iambic rhythm. And once/you start/you'll find/it hard/to stop!

'In a Railway Compartment' suggests that something alarming happens to the girl, but does not actually say so. It could all be the imagination at work. Notice the use of the word 'shrieking'. It obviously refers to the sound of the train as it enters the tunnel. But our minds cannot help seeing (or hearing) the other possibility, that it is the girl shrieking. This device of choosing words which can imply more than one meaning is a very important 'trick' in poetry. Can you think of a simple everyday situation you could describe? And without saying too much, can you describe it in such a way that a sinister note creeps in? You might think of it as trying to use language to create an atmosphere, in the same way that music is used in films to build up tension. You play on the feelings of your readers by carefully suggesting a danger that may, or may not, be there.

'In a Railway Compartment' is a sonnet. A sonnet is a form consisting of fourteen lines, all iambic pentameters and keeping to a fixed rhyme scheme. There are different sonnet rhyme patterns, and poets also make up their own variations. Generally the sonnet can be considered in two sections: the first eight lines (the octet) and the second six (the sestet). The rhyme scheme of this sonnet is as follows: in the octet

a, b, b, a, a, c, c, a

and in the sestet

d, e, f, f, e, d

(These letters denote the words at the ends of the lines; where the letters are the same, the lines rhyme.)

Glossary

Cinquain: a five-line poem invented by the American poet Adelaide Crapsey. Each of the five lines has a set number of syllables — 2, 4, 6, 8, 2 — to make twenty-two syllables in all. The rhythm is basically iambic (page 110).

Couplets, rhyming: pairs of lines, of any length, which rhyme (pages 55, 84, 110, 118); *heroic*: pairs of lines, written in iambic pentameter, which rhyme (page 28). (*Couplet* = pair of lines)

Found poem: a poem taken straight from some written material already in existence (and not intended to be a poem) and set out as poetry (page 64).

Iambic pentameter: a line of poetry which has five feet (like five bars in music) and is written in iambic rhythm. There are ten syllables to every strict iambic pentameter, two to each foot (pages 28, 54, 55, 117).

Iambic rhythm: a 'limping' rhythm, where the heavy stress of the voice falls on the second syllable in a pair of syllables (or 'foot') (e.g. bĕsíde) (pages 28, 54, 75, 110, 116, 117).

Iambic tetrameter: a line of poetry which has four feet (similar to bars in music) and is written in iambic rhythm. There are eight syllables in a strict iambic tetrameter, two to each foot (page 84).

Metaphor: comparing one thing with another, but *not* using words of comparison such as 'like' or 'as'; saying one thing *is* something else (pages 74, 75, 100, 110).

Metrical foot: a group of syllables similar to one bar in music. 'Feet' set the rhythm of a poem. There are many different kinds of rhythmic feet, based on the number of syllables and whether they are stressed or not. (Stressed syllables are marked / and unstressed ˇ: an example is the word bĕsíde.)

Mnemonic: a device for helping you to remember something, often done in rhyme. For the fate of Henry VIII's six wives, say:

> Divorced, beheaded, died,
> Divorced, beheaded, survived.

And *R*ichard *O*f *Y*ork *G*ave *B*attle *I*n *V*ain gives you the seven colours of the rainbow (page 64).

Octet (also known as 'octave'): the first eight lines of a Petrarchan sonnet (named after the Italian poet Petrarch), following a particular rhyme scheme (see *Sonnet*) (page 117).

Parody: an imitation of the words or style of another author, usually to 'poke fun' at the author. The best parodies are often clever 'take-offs' of well-known poems or rhymes (page 101).

Quatrain: a stanza of four lines, rhymed or unrhymed (pages 28, 64, 75).

Rhyme, full: words that echo exactly the same sound (e.g. 'time' and 'rhyme'); *half*: words that echo *part* of the same sound (e.g. 'love' and 'live', 'made' and 'fate')(pages 27, 35).

Sestet: the last six lines of a Petrarchan sonnet (see *Sonnet*), following a particular rhyme scheme and often bringing to a conclusion the ideas 'set up' in the octet (see *Octet*)(page 117).

Sonnet: a fourteen-line poem, usually in iambic pentameters, written to a particular rhyme scheme of which there are different patterns. One of these, the Petrarchan Sonnet, rhymes as follows: a, b, b, a, a, b, b, a (octet), c, d, e, c, d, e (sestet). Another, the Shakespearean Sonnet, rhymes a, b, a, b, c, d, c, d, e, f, e, f, g, g (page 117).

Stanza: a group of lines of verse, whether rhymed or unrhymed, though the word is mostly used of those that are rhymed (a stanza is what most people would call a 'verse').

Surrealism: the workings of the unconscious mind expressed in art and literature; the sort of images and ideas that might occur in dreams or nightmares (pages 83, 54).

Syllable: the smallest part or unit of a word, similar to one beat in music (e.g. 'word' is one syllable, 'music' is two syllables, 'syllable' is three syllables)(page 110).

Symbolism: using an object to represent, or 'stand for', something else — that is, using a symbol (e.g. 'day' as a symbol for 'life' and 'night' as a symbol for 'death')(page 54).

Triplet: three successive lines that rhyme with each other (page 27).

Book List

The poets in these pages are the authors of numerous individual books of poetry. Here are the titles of some of them in case you would like to read more of their work. Those marked 'Y' are books written especially for younger readers; the others are principally for older readers.

Kit Wright: *Bump-Starting the Hearse* (Hutchinson)
The Bear Looked Over the Mountain (Salamander Imprint)

George Szirtes:
The Slant Door (Secker and Warburg)
November and May (Secker and Warburg)

Grace Nichols: *The Fat Black Woman's Poems* (Virago)

Edwin Morgan: *From Glasgow to Saturn* (Carcanet)

Vernon Scannell: *Winterlude* (Robson Books)
New and Collected Poems (Robson Books)

Alan Brownjohn: *Collected Poems* (Secker and Warburg)
Brownjohn's Beasts (Macmillan) (Y)

Pete Morgan: *The Grey Mare Being the Better Steed* (Secker and Warburg)
The Spring Collection (Secker and Warburg)

George MacBeth: *Poems from Oby* (Secker and Warburg)
The Long Darkness (Secker and Warburg)

John Birtwhistle: *Tidal Models* (Anvil)
Our Worst Suspicions (Anvil)

Ted Hughes: *Selected Poems* (Faber)
Season Songs (Faber) (Y)

John Mole: *In and Out of the Apple* (Secker and Warburg)
Feeding the Lake (Secker and Warburg)

John Fuller: *Selected Poems* (Secker and Warburg)
The Beautiful Inventions (Secker and Warburg)

Writers in Schools Scheme

You may like to take the opportunity of actually meeting poets in person. Most of these poets will visit schools, and this can be arranged under a special scheme administered by your Regional Arts Association. All the addresses for these associations may be found in *Meet and Write Book One*, or obtained from your local public library. Your teacher should be able to arrange these visits if you ask.

What does the scheme offer?

*Assistance towards the payment of a fee and expenses, of 50% or more.

*A chance to meet a writer in person and work with him or her.

*Advice on how to set up a session to make the most of such a visit.

What will the writer do?

This varies, and should be clearly agreed before the writer's visit. Possibilities include:

*Reading from his or her work, and answering questions about the poems, and the life and craft of a writer.

*A workshop led by the writer, with the members of the audience writing their own work and obtaining help and criticism for it.

*Lectures or lessons on any aspect of poetry (or other forms of writing) including historical periods (for example, metaphysical, romantic or modern poetry), on individual writers, and on the craft of writing.

*Judging poetry competitions.

Index

x

Acknowledgments

The publisher and editors would like to thank the following for permission to reproduce copyright material in this book.

Kit Wright poems: Penguin Books for 'Useful Person', 'The Song of the Whale', and 'How to Treat the House Plants', Kit Wright for 'Mirror Poem'

George Szirtes poems: Patricia Lee for 'The Equilibrist', George Szirtes for 'The Cold Weather Cat', 'Umbrellas' and 'A Small Girl Swinging'

Grace Nichols poems: Virago Press

Edwin Morgan poems: Carcanet Press Ltd

Vernon Scannell poems: Robson Books Ltd

Alan Brownjohn poems: Martin Secker & Warburg Ltd

Pete Morgan poems: Martin Secker & Warburg Ltd

George MacBeth poems: Anthony Shiel Associates Ltd for 'When I am Dead', 'The Red Herring' and 'Bats', George MacBeth for 'Snowdrops'

John Birtwhistle poems: Anvil Press for 'The Hitch-hiker's Curse on Being Passed by', John Birtwhistle for 'Riddle'

Ted Hughes poems: Faber & Faber

John Mole poems: Secker & Warburg Ltd for 'Song of the Diplomat', E.J. Marten for 'Bats', John Mole for 'Reflections' and 'First Snow'

John Fuller poems: John Fuller

Drawings on pages 10, 17, 34, 51, 68, 77, 97 and 113 are by Jane Cope, Linda Rogers Associates; Photo credits are as follows: p. 8, Kit Wright; p. 20, George Szirtes; p. 22, Stacey-Garrard Associates; p. 29, Grace Nichols; p. 36, Fay Godwin; p. 38, NASA and the Liverpool Museum; p. 41, Associated Newspapers Group; p. 46, Lisbeth H. Hansen; p. 56, Fay Godwin; p. 66, Pete Morgan; p. 76, Fay Godwin; p. 85, John Birtwhistle; p. 86, Martin Finn, Nance Fyson; p. 90, Fay Godwin; p. 102, John Mole; p. 108, Frank Greenaway; p. 112, Fay Godwin